from the Father's Heart

Rest & Reflection

DAILY DEVOTIONAL

*Tailored for Life's Seasons -
Emotionally & Spiritually*

MARIA KEAR

From the Father's Heart
Rest & Reflection - Daily Devotional
Tailored for Life's Seasons —
Emotionally and Spiritually.

Copyright © 2024 by Maria Kear
All rights reserved, including the right of
reproduction in whole or in part in any form.

First Edition November 2024

STM Press
  978-1-966240-01-3 (paperback)
  978-1-966240-00-6 (ebook)

All scripture references are from the New
Living Translation unless otherwise noted.

All word definitions were taken from the
Strong's Online Concordance unless
otherwise noted.

Designed by Suzanne Parrott
Cover Image created using Midjourney

NO AI TRAINING: Without in any
way limiting the author's [and publisher's]
exclusive rights under copyright, any use of
this publication to "train" generative artificial
intelligence (AI) technologies to generate text
is expressly prohibited. The author reserves
all rights to license uses of this work for
generative AI training and development of
machine learning language models.

Acknowledgements

I want to thank my 5 family – Jeff, Matthew, Katherine and Abigail (I'm the 5th) for always cheering me on when I have crazy ideas like writing my own books. Even if they think I'm weird, they still love me.

I want to thank Debra Rothrock and Angie Davidson for their eyes on the text when they had a moment to make sure my grammar and punctuation were in line.

I want to thank Suzanne Fyhrie Parrott for being my publishing partner and the one who made all the details come together so my voice could be heard in the earth.

Dedication

This book is dedicated to the current and future Jesus lovers who will never tire of reading God's Words or of hearing Him speak. To the ones who love and seek out adventure with Holy Spirit as guide and partner. To the ones who are not satisfied with only what this world offers, but long for news from their place of origin – Heaven. And to those brave enough to hug their Bibles to their chests with wide smiles and tear-stained faces. You have found your people!

Author's Note

The first book I learned to read was the King James Version of the Holy Bible. I was five years old when I picked up the book and just started reading. My mom told me that no one taught me to read, but that I just started reading one day.

When I asked her how that was possible, she replied that from the moment I came home from the hospital to live with her and my grandparents Wheeler in Meggett, SC, my granddaddy Wheeler read to me, making sure I could see each page and picture as he read. We believe that his gift of reading to me from day one prepared my brain to be an early and life-long lover of books, especially the Bible.

Thank you, Granddaddy Wheeler.

Day 1

Image Bearers are Culture Shapers

Genesis 1, 2 / Matthew 1:1-2:12 / Psalm 1 / Proverbs 1:1-6

As I read the scriptures for today, I noticed a few things. When God created the earth and everything in it, He also created Adam and Eve *in His image*. He intended for those who were created *in His image* (the image bearers) to be fruitful and multiply, to "fill the earth and govern it."

God created the Heavens and the earth, then he "decorated" with plants, animals, the sun, the moon, and the stars. What did God mean when He told us to "be fruitful and multiply. Fill the earth and govern it. Reign over the fish in the sea...?" Genesis 1:28

He meant for us to have children, lots of children, who would grow up and fill the earth. The kind rulers created more kind rulers so that we could govern everything God made.

Copy, paste, govern, repeat... until He returns.

Adam and Eve cared for the animals, planted gardens, and eventually raised a family. They met with God every day to enjoy that intimacy. The image bearers met with the One who created them. It probably felt like looking into a mirror.

How does one govern the earth as an image bearer?

Up until this point in history, Adam and Eve probably governed with grace, love, and laughter. I have often wondered if they were able to talk with the animals. Life is good; like one big, happy family. Adam and Eve are serving and caring for the animals, the plants, the trees – and maybe the animals, plants and trees were caring for Adam and Eve.

6

There was no hint that anything could spoil this beautiful existence – that anything could interrupt the relationship man had with God. They met face-to-face, they heard one another's voices, they saw one another's smiles. They probably laughed at each other's jokes.

I bet Adam raced with the cheetah, and probably won sometimes! Maybe God and man also raced one another, then laughed and patted each other on the back. What a beautiful existence God created for us in Eden.

And I believe He still has an Eden experience for us today. He still draws us into intimate fellowship with Himself. He still wants to laugh with us, cry with us, talk to us and listen to our hearts.

What would you like to tell Him today? What do you hear Him saying to you about how you are His Image bearer?

Day 2

Shrewd - Clever, Discerning Awareness

Genesis 3, 4 / Matthew 2:13-3:6 / Psalm 2 / Proverbs 1:7-9

"The serpent was the shrewdest
of all the wild animals the LORD God had made."
—Genesis 3:1 NLT

What a fascinating sentence! Does this mean all animals were created as shrewd, and that the serpent was most shrewd?

What does shrewd mean?

Shrewd is defined as "marked by clever, discerning awareness or given to wily and artful ways or dealing."

The conversation between the shrewd serpent and Eve must have been very convincing because Eve ate the fruit.

Eve believed that eating the fruit would make her wise or give her wisdom. Don't we also want wisdom? Don't we want answers for our lives? To know that we're doing the right things at the right time. Yes, we do; especially in the chaotic time we find ourselves living.

The good news is we as the people of God have an advantage when it comes to getting wisdom! God warned Joseph in a dream to run from Egypt to protect the child who Herod was still trying to kill. And if we're listening to the voice of God in a personal way, we will also have wisdom, direction, and these things might just save our lives!

Aren't we all trying to "win," to "get ahead?" I think we turn things upside down when we try to use our own (or the world's) wisdom.

8

What joy for all who take refuge in Him! Psalm 2:12b

Fear of the Lord is the foundation of true knowledge. Proverbs 1:7a

If you need wisdom, don't listen to the shrewd voice of the enemy in hopes that he'll offer something of value. Instead, while taking refuge in Christ, and honoring His beautiful name, ask Him for the answers you need.

What is it that you need wisdom for today? Ask Him to speak to you for your situation.

Day 3

Walk in Close Fellowship with God

Genesis 5-7 / Matthew 3:7-4:11 / Psalm 3 / Proverbs 1:10-19

Gen 5:22 After the birth of Methuselah, Enoch lived in close fellowship with God for another 300 years... Enoch lived 365 years, walking in close fellowship with God. Then one day he disappeared, because God took him.

Gen 6:9 Noah was a righteous man... he walked in close fellowship with God.

Matthew 3:8 Prove by the way you live that you have repented of your sins and turned to God.

These are the thoughts that caught my attention as I read through today's scriptures. Did you notice that both Enoch and Noah were said to have "walked in close fellowship with God"?

How do we know they did? What proof did God have of this?

Matthew 3:8 may offer a clue to help answer those questions. According to this verse, the proof of our walking in close fellowship with God is the way we live.

I love to break down word meanings from scripture and sometimes I'll do that using the Strong's Online Concordance at the Eliyah website. So, let's do that and see if we are offered a little more insight into this close fellowship with God because I want to walk with Him in this way!

Evidently walking closely with God lines up with the proof mentioned in Matthew 3:8, because when I looked up the word "walked" from both Genesis 5 and 6 in the concordance, I found one

10

meaning that reinforces that the way we live matters. That definition is "manner of life."

This reminds me of another scripture in Matthew 20:25-28, and I like this passage as read in The Passion Translation.

" . . . Kings and those with great authority in this world rule oppressively over their subjects, like tyrants. [26] But this is not your calling. You will lead by a completely different model. The greatest one among you will live as the one who is called to serve others, [27] because the greatest honor and authority is reserved for the one with the heart of a servant. [28] For even the Son of Man did not come expecting to be served by everyone, but to serve everyone, and to give his life in exchange for the salvation of many."

This is how we should walk through this earth throughout our lives - to serve others. And this is the heart of my calling as Still the Mom - to serve others and champion them to become all God has called them to be!

Are you walking in such a way as to serve others? It's a great question, and an even greater life-calling.

Please consider today who you might serve.

Day 4

But God Remembered Noah

Genesis 8-10 / Matthew 4:12-25 / Psalm 4 /Proverbs 1:20-23

Today's readings were so good! I love history, so the account of Noah preparing to exit the ark after about a year aboard is so interesting to me.

When I read the Bible, I try to put myself in the place of those I'm reading about, and I started to feel a little anxious thinking about Noah, his wife, his sons, and daughters-in-law, and all those animals together on a boat in the water for a YEAR. Whew. If I were Noah, I may have been going a little stir crazy by the time God told me to leave the boat.

I don't know that I would have waited for God to tell me to leave. I think I would have been at that window every day and testing the door to see if it would budge (remember, Genesis says God shut Noah, his family and all the animals into the ark). But Noah waited.

I guess he was used to listening to and obeying God, even when it made him unpopular. Imagine being a man who was talking about a flood when no one knew what that was. I'm sure they thought he was super weird! Until it started to rain . . .

After Noah and his family left the ark, God made them and all of us a promise – never to destroy the earth again with a flood.

And that makes me think of a verse I found in Psalm 4:3, which states, "The LORD set apart the godly for Himself. The LORD will answer when I call to Him."

That's exactly what God did by sharing His plans with Noah; He set the godly apart for Himself. And we can be assured that if we

12

are His, we are also set apart and that He will answer us when we call to Him (pray.)

The answers we receive may not be what we expected, but we can know that He loves us and that He will answer according to what He knows is best for us and according to what will bring Him glory.

Let's never forget that our lives are for the purpose of pointing to Him.

Today, as you're spending time with the Lord, keep in mind that He is "remembering" you as He did Noah (see Genesis 8:1). Turn your heart to Him, and as you do, say a prayer for our nation and our leaders that they will seek God's will and purpose.

Day 5

Unity Brings Power

Genesis 11:1-13:4 / Matthew 5:1-26 / Psalm 5 / Proverbs 1:24-28

The story of the tower of Babel is usually seen in a negative light and I understand it being so because the people were acting on their own plan instead of God's. But when I read the account today, I had an opposite thought regarding Genesis 11:6.

"Look!" [God] said. "The people are united, and they all speak the same language. After this, nothing they set out to do will be impossible for them!"

"Unity brings power" is the message I'm hearing in God's words regarding these people who had settled in Babylonia. Perhaps the body of Christ would benefit from finding a way to settle upon true unity. I sure don't have an answer as to how we'd accomplish that; other than perhaps aligning ourselves with the plan God has for our households, cities, states, and nations.

It's the remnant of the body of Christ that will make a difference in the earth because they know they are part of another kingdom, which is Heaven. Matthew 5 is filled with clues about the true people of God, or the remnant as I call them. What do they look like? What do they believe? Who are they?

Here are just a few descriptors:

They realize their need for God, they are humble, they long for justice, they are merciful, they are pure-hearted, they work for peace, they are persecuted for doing right. In addition, they are the salt of the earth, they bring awakening and truth to a dying world, they are

14

the light of the world, and the good they do points to the Father's glory.

And we can't point to the Father's glory unless we are walking according to His plan for us. Psalm 5:8 is a beautiful and short prayer to that end. "Lead me in the right path, O LORD, or my enemies will conquer me. Make your way plain for me to follow."

That is my prayer for you and me today. That we would be united, not only with one another, but more importantly with God's heart and plan.

What do you hear Him saying to you today about His plan?

Day 6

*Remembering the Victories Helps Us
Stand Firm as We Wait for The Promises*

Genesis 13:5-15:21 / Matthew 5:27-48 / Psalm 6 / Proverbs 1:29-33

"Blessed be God Most High,
who has defeated your enemies for you."
—Genesis 14:20

I love that!!

Sometimes we think we must fight for ourselves, but God makes it clear all throughout scripture that He is our defender, and that we are to stand still and see His salvation. His promises are true, and we can depend upon them. Abram is one example from scripture of someone who learned about God's promises as he and God walked through life together.

Speaking of Abram, God told Abram twice that he would give him many descendants; once when he compared those descendants in this way "like the dust of the earth," and the second time when He said, "Look up into the sky and count the stars if you can. That's how many descendants you will have!"

It wasn't until God's second declaration that it was said of Abram that he "believed God."

Sometimes we need to hear God's promises multiple times before faith is birthed!

God changed Abram's name to Abraham when He told him he would be the father of many nations. Abraham wasn't sure how this promise would be fulfilled because he and his wife Sarah were old

16

and past the time of having children. This was the first test of God's promise!

As promised, Sarah did get pregnant, and Isaac was born. The first part of God's promise was fulfilled! We know the rest of the story because from Isaac came Jacob (Israel) and Esau, and out of both of these men many nations came into being.

What has God promised you that you have not yet seen?

What has God promised you that you have already seen?

It's important to keep in mind both the seen and unseen promises, because remembering the victories and promises fulfilled helps us stand firm as we wait for the promises to come!

What promise are you remembering today that God has fulfilled?

What promise are you still waiting for?

Be blessed in both!

Day 7

Our Prayer Today

Genesis 16:1-18:15 / Matthew 6:1-24 / Psalm 7 / Proverbs 2:1-5

In Matthew we read The Lord's Prayer, and I want to take time today to explore these words because we need to continue in prayer for our families, our friends, and our nation.

"Our Father in Heaven, may your name be kept holy."

When we pray, we must first remember Who we are praying to; remember His character and nature. We must remember that He is good and that He hears us because we are His. The definition of the name "Father" is "God is called the Father of Christians, as those who through Christ have been exalted to a specially close and intimate relationship with God, and who no longer dread him as a stern judge of sinners but revere Him as their reconciled and loving Father." As we look to God as Father, we must not forget that He is also holy. The definition of holy is "separate from profane things and dedicated to God."

"May Your Kingdom come on earth, as it is in Heaven."

God's Kingdom is already fully established and operational both in Heaven and within us, and it is a perfect Kingdom. It's our privilege to bring Heaven into earth as ambassadors of Christ. The definition of Kingdom is "royal power, dominion, rule, the right or authority to rule, of the royal power and dignity conferred on Christians in the Messiah's Kingdom."

"Give us today the food we need, and forgive us our sins, as we have forgiven those who sin against us."

18

God knows what we need to live each day, so we should be content to live from what His hand brings us. We must daily remember to ask God for forgiveness. We must take no offense against ourselves, others, or Him; otherwise, He will not hear our prayers.

"And don't let us yield to temptation but rescue us from the evil one."

The enemy, the devil, is always trying to get us to agree with his kingdom, but we must be aware of his tricks and not be fooled by them. Temptation is defined as "a trial of man's fidelity, integrity, virtue, constancy." Our way out from the temptations of the devil is to pray God rescues us from the traps he tries to set.

I also love the following verse from Psalm 7:9, and I think it's a good prayer to pray today in addition to The Lord's Prayer above.

"End the evil of those who are wicked and defend the righteous. For you look deep within the mind and heart, O righteous God."

Praying scripture is very effective because we can know we're praying God's will and purpose.

What scripture are you praying today for your family, your friends, and your nation?

Day 8

Love One Another

Genesis 18:16-19:38 / Matthew 6:25-7:14 / Psalm 8 / Proverbs 2:6-15

Many people think the God of the Old Testament (which is, of course, also the God of the new) was harsh and filled only with wrath. If that were true, why would He have listened to Abraham and agreed to spare two sin-filled cities for the sake of 10 people?

If you know the story, you know that the city was so filled with wickedness, that only Abraham's nephew Lot, along with his wife and daughters were found and rescued from the destruction. Yes, there was destruction of evil, but don't forget there was rescue for God's people. And that is a clear picture of God's nature. He is both judgment and mercy / wrath and love.

In Matthew we are reminded that God cares for the wildflowers, but He cares for those who are His much more. And because He cares for us, we ought to care for others.

Matthew 7:12 says, "Do to others whatever you would like them to do to you."

Psalm 8 has a beautiful portion reminding us of how precious we are to God. "When I look at the night sky and see the work of your fingers – the moon and the stars you set in place – what are mere mortals that you should think about them, human beings that you should care for them?"

If we know the God who loves, ought we not also love each other?

1 John 4:7-8 tells us: "Beloved, let us love one another; for love is of God, and he who loves is born of God and knows God. He who does not love does not know God; for God is love."

It's not my responsibility to defend God's character; He does that all by Himself. But I can tell you that over my lifetime of knowing Him – since the age of five – I have known Him to be a loving Father who brought both gentle corrections, as well as great comfort.

I'm thankful I belong to Him!

Day 9

Actions Have a Language

Genesis 20-22 / Matthew 7:15-29 / Psalm 9:1-12 / Proverbs 2:16-22

When Abraham and Sarah both agreed to tell a little white lie to Abimelech about her being Abraham's sister, their lie brought on a dream of warning from God, Abimelech's anger, and restitution paid to Abraham for the wrong committed against them both.

Where is the line between truth and lie? I have friends who see no line, friends who love that blurry, gray part in the middle, and friends who have a dark, bold line. But I wonder what God thinks. I mean, Abraham was still called and blessed of God, even though he told this white lie not once, but twice!

Does that mean it's okay to lie, knowing God will forgive and still bless you?

The first line of Genesis Chapter 21 is interesting "The LORD kept His word . . ."

Hm. If God keeps His word, ought we keep ours?

All that said, this does not negate that Abraham was quick to obey God whenever God asked him for anything. All of us have areas that are not surrendered yet. It is important to continually look at our lives for areas that need a Holy Spirit invasion!

Matthew talks about being able to identify false prophets by their fruit. Verse 16 begins, "You can identify them by their fruit, that is, by the way they act."

If our words identify to whom we belong, we must certainly be circumspect about the words we choose to speak. And we do have a choice in what we say.

22

What we think is another topic altogether! Because what we believe becomes what we think which becomes what we say.

Matthew says we can identify people not only by their words, but also by their actions.

My friend Steven B recently quoted, "Your actions are speaking so loudly, I can't hear what you're saying." So true.

We're all a work in progress with some areas surrendered to God and other areas yet to be surrendered.

I choose to believe there is always grace for what's next!

Day 10

Follow the Pleasing Path

Genesis 23:1-24:51 / Matthew 8:1-17 / Psalm 9:13-20 / Proverbs 3:1-6

Today there is a two-verse passage I want to highlight, and it's well-known, but let's not miss the treasure it contains.

Proverbs 3:5-6 (The Amplified Bible):

"Trust in and rely confidently on the Lord with all your heart and do not rely on your own insight or understanding. In all your ways know and acknowledge and recognize Him, and He will make your paths straight and smooth [removing obstacles that block your way]."

Y'all know I love to break down scripture, so let's do that for these two beautiful verses to gain better understanding. The reason better understanding has value is it allows us to apply the Word to our own lives and walk according to the truth we've read.

Trust: To have confidence or be confident, to be bold, to be secure, to feel safe.

Heart: Our mind, will and understanding. Our soul, inclination, thinking, determination. The seat of our appetites, emotions, and passions.

Rely: Trust, support oneself

Understanding: Discernment

Acknowledge: To know, learn to know or perceive. To distinguish. To know by experience. To recognize, admit, confess.

24

Straight paths: Way of living, road that is level, lawful, pleasing, agreeable, approved, laid smoothly out.

These definitions from the Hebrew language help to "fatten" or broaden our understanding of these two verses. Sometimes I enjoy studying a few verses this way, then writing my own version. No, I'm not changing scripture; I'm understanding and consuming it for myself! Here's my "re-write":

I am confident, bold, and secure in the Lord, and I do this with all my understanding and determination. I will not trust my own discernment. In all my ways, I will seek to know, distinguish, and experience Him. And as I do this, He will make my way of living and the path I travel on pleasing and smooth.

That last part does not mean life will be a bowl of cherries! But it does mean He will be in the center of every circumstance and that brings me great comfort!

Did you have a favorite verse or two from today's reading? If so, feel free to study it out and do your own re-write!

Day 11

Rebekah's Blessing

Genesis 24:52-26:16 / Matthew 8:18-34 / Psalm 10:1-15 / Proverbs 3:7-8

Rebekah's blessing in Genesis, spoken over her by her family, falls right in line with the blessings God has already promised Abraham and his descendants. It's so exciting to me when I find myself walking along the path God so lovingly laid before me!

Here is Rebekah's blessing from Genesis 24:60:

"Our sister, may you become the mother of many millions!

May your descendants be strong and conquer the cities of their enemies."

The next sentence is pivotal. "Then Rebekah and her servant girls mounted the camels and followed the man."

Rebekah had to go with Abraham's servant to meet her destiny. Her destiny did not come to her. She had to act; she had to move away from all she had known to embrace the new adventure God was leading her toward.

I am reminded of a scripture in James. "Just as the body is dead without breath, so also faith is dead without good works," James 2:26.

Yes, we must have faith. Yes, we must pray.

But what are we going to do with what God is telling us?

I can't tell you what to do, but God sure can. If He's showing you a direction He wants you to go, what steps are you taking toward that?

I'm writing this book because I believe I heard God tell me to write! I want to do something with what God has spoken.

What about you? What has God said, and what are you doing to take steps toward that?

26

Day 12

Our Only Hope

Genesis 26;17-27:46 / Matthew 9:1-17
Psalm 10:16-18 / Proverbs 3:9-10

Between yesterday's devotional and today's, we have experienced the sudden passing of our future son-in-law, so some of my posts may reflect the grief we are walking through. Of course, as with all of life, all the emotions will be experienced and shared. We covet your continued prayers for our family and his. This is the great loss of an extremely gentle and beautiful soul, and we were blessed to have him as part of our family.

In Matthew 9:6 it says, "I want you to know that the Son of Man has authority on earth to forgive sins."

And later in verse 12 it says, "It is not the healthy who need a doctor, but the sick."

What great hope and promise of new and better days these two verses offer! Some of us think our sins define us, both for today and for the future, but I strongly argue for the opposite. There is forgiveness through Jesus Christ!

And to whom was Jesus referring when he mentioned the sick? He was referencing those with whom He was choosing to spend time – the tax collectors and sinners. He understood where the need was, and He went straight to the heart of that need.

We must do the same. We must love and have compassion for those who have not yet seen the Hope.

Psalm 10:17 says, "You, LORD, hear the desire of the afflicted; you encourage them, and you listen to their cry, defending the fatherless and the oppressed."

28

When life seems hard, when hope has disappeared, God is always there with His Spirit to comfort us and give us strength for today. And that is our only hope in hard times!

Regarding Bradley's passing, my beautiful aunt asked, "How does one get past this?"

My answer was, "Jesus is our only hope of moving beyond this. Nothing in us can fix what has happened, or we could have saved Bradley."

Her response was, "Wise words. She's (our daughter Abigail) lucky to have you!"

And that's the truth. Nothing in us can save those we love. Each of us must depend on the gift of salvation that Jesus provides.

Please depend on Him today.

In Loving Memory of Bradley Joseph Schultz
April 30, 1993 – January 11, 2021

Until we meet again...

Day 13

Life Here to Life There

Genesis 28-29 / Matthew 9:18-38 / Psalm 11 / Proverbs 3:11-12

In Matthew verses 23-25 we see Jesus going to visit a young girl who has died, and I love his bold response. He had knowledge that those in the house did not have; namely, that God was going to give this young girl her life again.

And that is just what Jesus did for us. Jesus said, "The girl isn't dead; she's only asleep." (Verse 24)

We may be dead in our sins, but if we hear the voice of Christ, He will rescue us from the wages of sin, which are death.

For the believer, there is no death. We leave life here and enter Heaven and eternal life with our Creator and Father.

When my dad died in October 2016, the grief was overwhelming, but God gave me a revelation that helped so much, and I've clung to that. He shared with me that my daddy didn't die (at least not according to the way the world understands). No. My daddy went from life on earth to life with Jesus Christ.

As we mourn the loss of our future son-in-law, I remember Jesus's words to me and say to myself once again, Bradley did not die – he passed from life on earth to life in the arms of his Heavenly Father.

What beauty he is seeing now!

"In the LORD I take refuge."
—Psalm 11:1

30

Day 14

Freely Give Away What You Have

Genesis 30:1-31:16 / Matthew 10:1-23 / Psalm 12 / Proverbs 3:13-15

Each day before I read, I ask the Lord to help me see what He wants me to see. Some days it's many thoughts and some days it's few; some days many words, and some days few. Today, one phrase grabbed my heart as I read and asked God what He had for me.

> "Give as freely as you have received!"
> —Matthew 10:8b

But how many are willing to do that? I've met some of the most generous people in my lifetime so far, and I've also met some very self-centered people. At this point in life, I've learned to gravitate toward the generous and away from the selfish.

My family has lived a long life of giving freely – all of us! We learned it from my parents, and Jeff and I passed this to our children and now this "freely give" heart posture is being passed to our grandchildren. Because as followers of Jesus, there is no other way to live.

Now, that does not mean we don't have boundaries. Oh, we do! Thus, the reason I find myself gravitating toward some people and away from others. I much prefer to invest in strong, healthy relationships where there is giving and receiving on both sides of the conversation. As a matter of fact, you won't likely find me investing otherwise.

What have I been freely given that I want to freely give? Love. Acceptance. Forgiveness. Understanding. Compassion. A listening

32

ear. Advice when asked for. Laughter. Boundaries. The list could go on and on because we are rich in the areas that matter most!

What have you been freely given? And what might you be able to freely give today?

Ask God for His input on this question and get out there and give your life away. I say there is no other way to live.

Day 15

Unfailing Love

Genesis 31:17-32:12 / Matthew 10:24-11:6
Psalm 13 / Proverbs 3:16-18

In Genesis 32:10 Jacob said to God, "I am not worthy of all the unfailing love and faithfulness you have shown to me, your servant."

Matthew 10:29-31, "What is the price of two sparrows – one copper coin? But not a single sparrow can fall to the ground without your Father knowing it. And the very hairs on your head are all numbered. Don't be afraid; you are more valuable to God than a whole flock of sparrows."

Psalm 13: 5-6, "But I trust in Your unfailing love. I will rejoice because you have rescued me. I will sing to the LORD because He is good to me."

These are the verses that spoke to my heart today. Yes, we're grieving, but scripture tells us that those who belong to Jesus don't grieve as the world does because we have hope. So, while we grieve, we also trust. While our hearts are broken, we know God is working to mend them.

And the truth is God's unfailing love has been abundant not only now, but also all my life! Yes, there are hard things, and everyone experiences those hard things. But most of my life has been filled with sweetness and blessings.

I have an amazing, close-knit family – as a matter of fact, as I type this, we're all bunked up together to support Abigail and each other and we'll do that as long as needed because that's what we do!

34

No matter the sorrow, I trust His love that doesn't fail. I trust that He sees each of our hurting hearts, and I trust that He is sad with us.

But there is another side to our sorrow, and that is the joy of knowing that Bradley's suffering has ended and that he is in Heaven. Parallel to our joy is the fact that we will walk through this time and come to the other side where we'll remember that God is always good.

I'm thankful for His unfailing love.

Day 16

Our Names Speak Destiny

Genesis 32:13-34:31 / Matthew 11:7-30 / Psalm 14 / Proverbs 3:19-20

As Jacob wrestled with God, not willing to give up until God blessed him, his name was changed. He went from being Jacob the supplanter (to supersede (another) especially by force or treachery) to Israel (God prevails).

Was there anyone else in scripture whose name was changed? There were several, but I want to focus only on those whose names were changed by God.

Abram (exalted father) became Abraham (father/chief of a multitude).

Sarai (princess) became Sarah (noblewoman).

Lo-Ammi (not my people) was renamed Ammi (my people).

Lo-Ruhamah (no love or mercy) was renamed Ruhamah (to love deeply or have mercy).

Pashhur (freedom) was renamed Magor-missabib (Terror on Every Side).

Simon (a rock or stone) was renamed Peter (stone).

Saul (desired) was renamed Paul (small or little).

36

As I ponder what it means to have your name changed – either by God, another person or yourself, I wonder what that means for our destiny?

Maybe you've heard the story of how I got my name. If not, in short, my dad named me long before he and my mom were married. He knew his first child would be a daughter, and her name would be Maria. The name Maria has many meanings, but for this entry, that doesn't matter much.

Our names mark our destiny. They are an intrinsic identity that causes us to think of ourselves in a certain way – to carry ourselves through life a certain way. Much like the words of others can either encourage or derail our destiny, our names will do the same.

There is another "naming" that is even more important than our first names, and that is any name the Lord places on us as His people.

We are His treasured possessions, beloved, kings and priests, His bride, a holy temple, a remnant, a vessel unto honor, the apple of His eye and many more. All the titles He calls us by are given with affection because He loves us so much.

God does everything with purposeful intention. He calls us what He does to set destiny, hope, and purpose into our hearts. He names us for our success in His Kingdom and for His glory.

Day 17

Walk With...

Genesis 35-36 / Matthew 12:1-21 / Psalm 15 / Proverbs 3:21-26

Psalm 15 is interesting because the text helps us discern who are those that follow Christ. How? Let's look!

"Who may worship in Your sanctuary, Lord? Who may enter Your presence on Your holy hill? Those who lead blameless lives and do what is right, speaking the truth from sincere hearts" (Verses 1-2).

You probably know what's coming – a closer look at some word meanings!

Lead = manner of life

Blameless = wholesome, unimpaired, innocent, what is complete or entirely in accord with truth and fact

Do what is right = as ethically right

Speaking the truth = declares spoken truth

Sincere hearts = the character of the man as said to himself in his own heart

Did anyone else catch that last part? When we think about speaking the truth, we think of words and sounds coming out of our mouths, but this verse says that we can "speak truth in our hearts."

It is our responsibility to encourage ourselves in our faith. Yes, there are times when we need the help of others. Sometimes life is overwhelming; it's great to have others who are like-minded to help

38

us in those times. However, most of our courage will come from the words we feed ourselves and the thoughts we ponder.

Before a word comes out of our mouths, a thought is formed. Before a thought is formed, a worldview must be built and that comes from our life experiences and from the input we choose. What are we reading, watching and listening to?

If what we believe brings life, that's good. If our beliefs build a false narrative, we must at some point challenge what we believe. If we are going to speak the truth to our own hearts, so that what comes out of our mouths is helpful, we must study to find that solid truth.

Some of you are wondering where you would find the truth. I know of only one text that contains tested thoughts and ideas, and that is the Bible, which is God's inspired Word. Solely reading the Bible doesn't always allow us to come away with a solid foundation. We must also ask the Holy Spirit to bring understanding.

There is one helpful scripture I want to share with you, one that you can use to measure what you hear, read and see.

Philippians 4:8 "And now, dear brothers and sisters, one final thing. Fix your thoughts on what is true, and honorable, and right, and pure, and lovely, and admirable. Think about things that are excellent and worthy of praise."

If we use this verse as a measuring stick for what we allow as input into our hearts, we will build a firmer foundation as well as a strong building. Christ is the foundation, and we are the building. Let's discern and use the proper materials.

Finally, if you find yourself wanting to walk (manner of life) according to the guidelines in Philippians 4:8, it's likely that you are in Christ, or you are at least wanting to head that direction.

39

Day 18

Hopes, Fears, Dreams

Genesis 37-38 / Matthew 12:22-45 / Psalm 16 / Proverbs 3:27-32

Have you ever shared a dream, hope or fear with a family member or friend only to be made fun of? I'm sure we all have, and I'm sure we remember the sting of it. Some of us when stung for the first time, clam up and refuse to share further. Others of us will share again, hoping to be received differently. I've done both.

And that's part of the pain and frustration of relationships. We want to share our hearts with others, but when we do, we're taking the risk of being hurt or rejected. So, what should we do?

While I can't really tell you whether to share or not, I can tell you that when God gives you something for yourself, you must decide in wisdom and discernment whether to share. Not everyone is ready to hear what you have to say. Sometimes a "wait and see" approach is best.

Joseph in the Bible was young and impulsive, so he kept sharing his dreams and it got him sold into slavery! If you know the rest of the story, you know God used his situation to save his family, and his dreams literally came true. But the family also suffered many years of estranged relationships, and Joseph's father thought he was dead.

Jesus was also falsely accused and misunderstood. He was accused of casting out demons by demons. They basically accused Him of being on the wrong team. He was the Son of God and was accused of being in league with the devil. His response was to speak truthfully to the religious leaders who didn't know who He was.

I also think about Mary when she became aware in Luke 2:19 what was being said about her newborn Jesus. The prophets, the angels, the shepherds – many knew who He was - but she took the words and kept them within her heart. She chose not to share what God was revealing and allowed the story of Jesus' life to unfold and be the proof of what she was hearing.

What about you? What has God shown you about your life? How have you chosen to process that? Have you shared it with everyone? A few trusted friends or family members? Or have you kept it to yourself?

I pray God gives you wisdom and discernment concerning when to speak and when to stay quiet, waiting for Him to unfold the plan He has revealed.

Day 19

Hidden Preparation

Genesis 39:1-41:16 / Matthew 12:46-13:23
Psalm 17 / Proverbs 3:33-35

Let's talk about Joseph again today. It's interesting that the dreamer has now become a dream interpreter. It also seems as if he's been humbled during his time in captivity and prison.

I don't know how many years Joseph was held in Egypt, but it was a time of hidden preparation for the things God had called him to do. However, even in the time of preparation, God used him.

There is not a time in our lives, even the hidden times, when God is not speaking, requiring something from us and using us to advance His plan. So be on the lookout for what He has for you to do!

That said, I'm sure Joseph went through a gambit of emotions from anger to frustration, from sadness to despair, from hope to fear.

In reading Psalm 17, I wonder if Joseph's prayers to God during his time in prison sounded a little like this chapter.

Did you know praying the Psalms can be powerful? If you're ever at a loss regarding what to pray, choose an appropriate Psalm!

"O LORD hear my plea for justice. Listen to my cry for help. Pay attention to my prayer, for it comes from honest lips. Declare me innocent, for you see those who do right." Psalm 17:1-2

There is much more in the Psalm which would have been appropriate for Joseph to have prayed.

Please go finish reading it and see if there is something in there for you! If you read some words that touch your heart, imagine yourself in the text and pray it out loud to God. He will hear you, and He will answer!

42

Day 20

Are You the Wheat?

Genesis 41:17-42 / Matthew 13:24-46 / Psalm 18:1-15 / Proverbs 4:1-6

The parable of the wheat and the weeds is being played out on the earth today. Both the wheat and the weeds have been planted together and the Lord is separating the two, proving who belongs to Him and who does not. Beware, this is no bedtime story; this is stark truth.

"Sir, the field where you planted that good seed is full of weeds! Where did they come from?"

"An enemy has done this!" the farmer exclaimed.

"Should we pull out the weeds?" they asked.

"No," he replied, "you'll uproot the wheat if you do. Let both grow together until the harvest. Then I will tell the harvesters to sort out the weeds, tie them into bundles, and burn them, and to put the wheat in the barn." Matthew 13:27-29

If you watch the news, or read the paper, or hop onto social media to see what's happening in the world, you are aware that God is highlighting His people, His Church, His Remnant in this season in history. Evil is becoming more apparent, but remember that when darkness threatens to overtake, that is when the light of God shines brightest through His people!

If you continue reading in Matthew, you'll see who the wheat represents and who the weeds represent. I encourage you to plant yourself in the field of wheat. If you don't know how to do that, reach out to a friend who follows Jesus and ask.

44

I want to end with Psalm 18:1-3.

"I love you, LORD; you are my strength. The LORD is my rock, my fortress, and my savior; my God is my rock, in whom I find protection. He is my shield, the power that saves me, and my place of safety. I called on the LORD who is worthy of praise, and he saved me from my enemies."

The people of God will always find hope and help in Him.

Day 21

Rescue

Genesis 42:18-43:34 / Matthew 13:47-14:12
Psalm 18:16-36 Proverbs 4:7-10

There were two verses in today's reading that grabbed my heart and attention, and they are similar in feel and meaning to me.

"The Kingdom of Heaven is like a fishing net that was thrown into the water and caught fish of every kind." —Matthew 13:47

"He reached down from Heaven and rescued me;
He drew me out of deep waters."
—Psalm 18:16

A net of fish of every kind speaks of all men and women being drawn in, so a global rescue. Conversely, in Psalm 18 it gets personal; He is rescuing me.

And that is the heart of God for all people. His heart is both to rescue nations and to rescue you and me.

Look at these verses from 2 Peter 3:8-9, "But you must not forget this one thing, dear friends; a day is like a thousand years to the Lord, and a thousand years is like a day. The Lord isn't really being slow about his promise, as some people think. No, he is being patient for your sake. He does not want anyone to be destroyed but wants everyone to repent."

God threw out the "big net" when he died on the cross, resurrected from the dead, then ascended into Heaven – everyone is offered the gift of salvation, then when time has ended on earth, the separation will begin between those who said "yes" and those who said "no" to God's free gift. (see Matthew 13:48-51)

As the separation begins, like we talked about with the wheat and the weeds (or chaff), everyone is separated as either wicked or righteous. What are the criteria?

There is only one criterion. The Son. Jesus Christ. Did you say, "Yes," or did you say, "No?" Did you receive or reject His gift of salvation?

It's never too late – at least as long as you're alive. So, if you have not yet said "yes", please say a prayer of "I believe."

Day 22

My Warrior Spirit

Genesis 44-45 / Matthew 14:13-36 / Psalm 18:37-50 / Proverbs 4:11-13

> "I chased my enemies and caught them; I did not
> stop until they were conquered. I struck them down so
> they could not get up; they fell beneath my feet."
> —Psalm 18:37-38

Are y'all ready to see my warrior side? Ready or not, here I come!

Those verses above and the ones that follow fire me up! If you met me, you would say that I appear to be a mild-mannered momma and Gigi, and I am. But there's also a no-nonsense, don't mess with me or my people side. Once I know you are part of my people, watch out if anyone tries to mess with you.

I think it's important to look at who our enemies are. As Christians we have one great enemy who is always trying to weasel his way in to steal our stuff, kill our dreams and destroy our faith. The other aspect is that he works through people.

The Bible says we don't fight with flesh and blood, but with principalities and powers (evil spirits.) That's true. But I'm allowed to distance myself from people who are ruled by those spirits. I don't have to allow any and every person into my space. And neither do you!

But neither do I get to think about people when I read those verses from Psalm 18. But I can sure as heck think about chasing

48

down and conquering in prayer those evil spirits who are bothering my people and me. I'm going to make them pay. But how?

With worship, praise, and prayer. Little "d" hates all these... (that's how I refer to the enemy, the devil. He's also "little s.")

There is one more powerful weapon when we are standing against the enemy and that is forgiveness. Sometimes it's hard to separate the fact that people are not our enemies. So, when the enemy is attacking us through those we love, our best defense is to forgive those who hurt us.

Is there anyone today that you have not forgiven? If you're unsure, say a quick prayer to ask. God will show you and you'll have an opportunity to walk away with a lighter heart.

Day 23

Sweeter Than Honey

Genesis 46-47 / Matthew 15:1-28 / Psalm 19 / Proverbs 4:14-19

"They are more desirable than gold, even the finest gold.
They are sweeter than honey, even honey
dripping from the comb."
—Psalm 19:10

What are they? What could possibly be more valuable than gold and sweeter than honey?

I want to highlight a few more verses from Psalm 19, so we can answer those last questions.

7 "The instructions of the LORD are perfect, reviving the soul. The decrees of the LORD are trustworthy, making wise the simple.

8 "The commandments of the LORD are right, bringing joy to the heart. The commands of the LORD are clear, giving insight for living.

9 "Reverence for the LORD is pure, lasting forever. The laws of the LORD are true; each one is fair."

Some think that following rules, commands, laws, etc. is tedious and constricting. And I get that. I tend to be a little bit of a hippie myself, and I don't like rules that box me in or steal my creativity.

But what if God's rules are different?

50

I love to call God's Kingdom the Upside-Down Kingdom. Why? Because everything there is totally opposite of everything here.

I was talking to my daughter and her friend recently and telling them how there is no way we can comprehend Heaven with our human mind. Nothing in our humanity understands God.

If you've ever read John's descriptions in Revelation, you'll see that describing Heaven is all but impossible. So why would we read the Bible and try to understand it from a human perspective?

To understand the Bible, we must allow the Holy Spirit to reveal the truth to us. To me, that's the beginning of a great adventure! I can't simply apply my mind to understand. I must dig out the truth of the Bible like I would gold. And the value of that truth lasts far beyond this world. I'll get to keep these treasures forever.

In answer to the questions above, the things that are more desirable than gold and sweeter than honey are His instructions, His commandments, our reverence for Him, and His laws. Now that we may see them differently, the gold and sweetness can be ours!

What do you think of the Upside-Down Kingdom? Is it real? What have been your experiences of Heaven and His truth?

Day 24

Bread or Grace?

Genesis 48-49 / Matthew 15:29-16:12 / Psalm 20 / Proverbs 4:20-27

"Later, after they crossed to the other side of the lake, the
disciples discovered they had forgotten to bring any bread.
'Watch out!' Jesus warned them. 'Beware of the yeast of the
Pharisees and Sadducees.' At this they began to argue with each
other because they hadn't brought any bread."
—Matthew 16:5-7

I can understand the disciples being confused about this whole
exchange of words. I have a feeling I also would have jumped straight
to thoughts of not having brought bread for our journey!

However, Jesus is not talking about food. What is Jesus warning
the disciples about? He's warning about religious, empty teachings.
But teachings about what?

From an online Bible history document – "the main downfall of
the Pharisees was in not following the principles that they themselves
taught but they made the Law a burden with their oral traditions."

As for the Sadducees, well they were "sad, you see." Sorry, I
couldn't resist, lol!

Seriously, what did they teach that we should avoid?

They taught that men's traditions and justification by the Law
were what made us right with God. We are instead justified by our
faith in Jesus Christ. Justification is defined as "to pronounce righteous or acceptable," according to Strong's Online Concordance.

The religious leaders also taught that there was no resurrection from the dead, which totally negates Jesus's death, burial, and resurrection. They taught many more things which you could study and find on your own.

What should we believe and teach instead of these false ideologies? Jesus taught many times about the Gospel of the Kingdom. He taught us that the Kingdom is at hand and is inside of us.

We must not put rules on ourselves or others: we must allow Holy Spirit to speak and change us into the image of Jesus. After all, that is what we are predestined for – to be conformed into His image.

If you wish to study further, read Matthew, Mark, Luke, and John, and become aware of how Jesus lived His life. He is an example to us of how we should live in a relationship with the Father and with each other.

Let's be people of great love and compassion just as Jesus was.

Day 25

Listen to Him!

Genesis 50:1-Exodus 2:10 / Matthew 16:13-17:9
Psalm 21 / Proverbs 5:1-6

There were so many fascinating and interesting portions in my reading today, but one passage in Matthew stood out more than the rest. I've been thinking a lot lately about how important it is to align my ways with God's ways.

Unfortunately, there are many voices in the world today, and they are all saying so many different things. Which of these voices is speaking the truth? How do I know to whom or to what I should listen?

Honestly, I've had to forego most of what comes my way, both because it's overwhelming, but also because I am searching hard to find God's voice in all the noise! That's why several verses in Matthew caught my attention.

Matthew 16:21-23 is a familiar passage, but Jesus's words may seem harsh because of the way He speaks to Peter. However, His words were necessary for Peter and for us to hear. I want to focus on two phrases.

The first from Matthew 16:23b - "You are seeing things merely from a human point of view, not from God's."

And second from Matthew 17:5, "This is my dearly loved Son, who brings me great joy. Listen to Him."

Are you interested in simplifying your life? Do you want to reduce anxiety, fear, and dread? Then I encourage you to listen to the voice of the Spirit of God!

54

Turn off the TV. Turn off the radio. Tune into the Holy Spirit. What is He saying to you as His dearly loved son or daughter? I promise you there is no fear in what He says. I promise you there is hope in what He says.

And that is what we all need right now. We must not come into alignment with either the kingdoms of this world or the kingdom of the enemy, satan. And trust me, these kingdoms have a message to share.

Choose the message and voice of truth. It may take active and fierce discipline to do this, but you will thank yourself for the effort!

Today, I pray that all voices except the voice of your Father in Heaven will be silenced. I pray the Father's voice cuts through all others and brings you the hope and peace we all so desperately need right now.

Day 26

Fight for the Promise

Exodus 2:11-3:22 / Matthew 17:10-27
Psalm 22:1-18 / Proverbs 5:7-14

The stories in both Genesis and Exodus cover many hundreds of years. We've gone from the excitement of Abram being called by God to go to a land God promised to give him to several generations later and the people of God still do not possess what God promised.

I'd also say God's people living in Goshen in Egypt have likely forgotten God's promise of a "land flowing with milk and honey."

Do you sometimes feel it's taking way too long to see the promise of God? Well, you're in good company! And it's not over yet for you or for the people we are reading about in the Bible!

Pharaoh will say "no" to God and to Moses, then he will finally relent and let God's people leave Egypt, then he and his army will chase God's people into the desert. Next, God's chosen people will wander for 40 years... But let's save those stories for another day.

Today I want to talk about the fact that the land of promise is filled with nations of giants. God has not yet told the people that they'll have to fight to acquire what God has promised. Maybe if He had told them about the fight upfront, they would have been terrified, so He doesn't give them that information until the time comes to fight.

What has God promised you? Have you been through the testing yet? Have you been through the process of removing the giants, so you can have what God promised?

56

I don't know where you are in your story but be assured God has not forgotten what He said. He still intends to bless you, but you may have to fight! And we certainly don't fight the way the world does.

We don't grab our guns, put up our fists, etc. No, we worship, and we pray. And these "weapons of our warfare" are mightier than any earthly weapon, gaining for us eternal treasure.

So, don't give up and don't give in - keep fighting. Stand strong like Ephesians 6:10 says! And when you feel weary, find a friend who will remind you of the good things God has for you.

Day 27

Is the Bible Funny?

Exodus 4:1-5:21 / Matthew 18:1-20 / Psalm 22:19-31 / Proverbs 5:15-21

Today's reading caught the attention of my humorous side! Sometimes when I'm reading, I put myself into the scene trying to imagine what it must have looked like. We can tend to read the Bible, putting a "holy" spin on it, but the truth is the people in the Bible were just like us!

They got angry, sad, did stupid things, etc. I bet they even rolled their eyes!

The funny part in today's reading was when God told Moses to throw his staff down on the ground and it became a snake. I would have been running and screaming! What did Moses do? He jumped back.

Imagine Moses at about 80 years old by now. He sees his staff turn into a snake and jumps back! I was laughing as I read this! I couldn't help it. This was hilarious to me. I wonder what his face looked like. I wonder if he screamed like a girl.

The point of today's entry is what I mentioned above. The people in the Bible were just like us. They were living the story as it unfolded and someone (several people) wrote the history down for all of us to read.

What might your story look like? I'm sure it would be a combination of ups and downs, highs, and lows. You know – the good, the bad and the ugly. We all have that in our stories, contrary to the personas we have created on social media.

That leads me to an appeal that we be real in our relationships

58

with others. I'll say it again, we've been walking through a season of terrible loss and grief. No one says we're doing it perfectly, but one thing we're not doing is ignoring it. No, we're talking about it every day.

That's something we must do; process the things we're going through. We cannot stuff down our emotions and feelings and expect to be healthy.

If you have anything unprocessed emotionally today, I pray you're able to talk to someone about it and get some healing for your soul.

Day 28

He is Coming!

Exodus 5:22-7:25 / Matthew 18:21-19:12 / Psalm 23 / Proverbs 5:22-23

Imagine yourself a prisoner in a foreign land who has been forced into slave labor. Your family has been in this situation for many generations. Maybe you have no idea that freedom is possible. Maybe you do have hope that someone will come to rescue you and your family. Then someone does come, and you're expecting immediate release from your slavery; however, things get worse, and you begin to think freedom is not possible after all.

That is what it sometimes feels like as we pray and wait for God to answer. We may be experiencing a devastating situation in our own life, or in the lives of our family or friends, and we begin to wonder if God is listening. I can assure you He is. But His timing is never the same as ours. Why?

I don't have that answer, except in principle. Everything in our lives is meant to reveal the love and glory of God, even the difficult places. That's part of why I love Psalm 23 so much.

Psalm 23 is not meant to be read in a void; it's meant to be taken to heart in both the good and the tough times.

"The Lord is my Shepherd and I have everything I need!" Try saying that when your life is so dark you can't see the light at the end!

"He lets me rest in green meadows; he leads me beside peaceful streams. He renews my strength. He guides me along right paths, bringing honor to His name." Imagine doing this when there is a tornadic storm surrounding your life!

"Even when I walk through the darkest valley, I will not be

60

afraid, for you are close beside me. Your rod and your staff protect and comfort me." The hard times must come, but God is always with us, guiding us through that dark valley!

"You prepare a feast for me in the presence of my enemies. You honor me by anointing my head with oil. My cup overflows with blessings." Now we're talking. My enemies must sit and watch me be blessed even as I wait for the answer to my prayers to come – even as I'm being assailed by attacks and difficulties. There is hope!

"Surely your goodness and unfailing love will pursue me all the days of my life, and I will live in the house of the LORD forever."

So, if you're praying, waiting, feeling discouraged, or have lost your courage or hope, read this Psalm repeatedly. It offers the boldness you need to stay the course as you wait for the goodness of God to be poured out over your life!

What if life doesn't look like you expected it to?
Stand firm anyway!

What if it looks like evil is winning?
Stand firm anyway!

What if all you're hearing is bad news?
Stand firm anyway!

God is good, and He is coming!

Day 29

Open Up, Ancient Doors

Exodus 8-9 / Matthew 19:13-30 / Psalm 24 / Proverbs 6:1-5

Has any of you noticed as you read the Exodus account of the plagues that the first three affected God's people, but the last seven did not? I can't tell you why God allowed the first three to affect them, but I do find it interesting that as God is showing Himself powerful among the Egyptians, as He is working through Moses to free His people from slavery, He is creating a division between those who are His and those who are not.

Sometimes as God's people we're affected by all the things in the world, and sometimes God spares us. It will be interesting to get to Heaven one day and see how much He kept from coming our way simply because we belong to Him. I have a feeling it's more than we realize.

Some don't understand how a loving God would allow suffering. God gave us free will to do as we choose. Evil is present, and it is evil that affects our world and the people in it with suffering and pain. This is a temporary condition though because in Heaven there will be no more pain!

I've been pondering our role in governing the earth. The Lord and I have been talking about the fact that it is our job as the Church to bring the influence of Heaven's realm into our reality. We are meant to show the love of Jesus, to be those who stand in the gap for our families, friends, and our nation.

I wonder if the world might look different had we fully understood our role. Would we have been able to negate some of that pain

62

and suffering by being God's conduits? I think it would be fascinating to find out!

Psalm 24 tells us that the earth is the Lord's. It tells us that He is strong and mighty, invincible in battle. Verse 9 states, "Open up, ancient doors, and let the King of glory enter."

What if we are those ancient doors that are to open and allow the King of glory to enter our lives and bear influence around us? If we're in Christ, we are carriers of His presence and glory. Do we hide that presence, or do we release it on the earth around us?

Today, I'm attempting to cause you to think – to ask God what your role on the earth is to be. Lord, am I a door for your presence on the earth? Is my door open so that others may receive from You?

I encourage you to open your door and let the King of glory enter through you!

Day 30

I Give My Life to You

Exodus 10:1-12:13 / Matthew 20:1-28 / Psalm 25:1-15 / Proverbs 6:6-11

While Jesus's disciples were fighting for position and recognition, I wonder what He was thinking. I think He probably smiled to Himself, seeing their imperfect human hearts and desires, but I also think He had compassion for their ignorance. They didn't yet understand how the Upside-Down Kingdom worked.

They were used to having to put themselves forward to earn favor with leaders or earn a living for their families. And we still do the same things. We still contend in this world for what we already possess through Jesus Christ in His Kingdom.

In verses 26-28 of Matthew it says, "But among you it will be different. Whoever wants to be a leader among you must be your servant, and whoever wants to be first among you must become your slave. For even the Son of Man came not to be served but to serve others and to give His life as a ransom for many."

When I read that Jesus came not to be served but to serve, my heart is reminded of the humility we must walk in as His followers. I don't need a name for myself. I don't need fame or notoriety, at least not according to this world. If I want true fame, true treasure, true abundant life, I must volunteer my life in service of God and others.

Let this be our prayer:

"O LORD, I give my life to you. I trust in you, My God!"
—Psalm 25:1-2a

64

Day 31

Ask Seek Knock

Exodus 12:14-13:16 / Matthew 20:29-21:22
Psalm 25:16-22 Proverbs 6:12-15

Did anyone else notice this tiny exchange in today's reading? There are two blind men who were sitting beside the road. They heard that Jesus was coming and began shouting for Jesus to have mercy on them. When the crowd yelled at them to be quiet, they "only shouted louder."

Several observations: first, these men could not see but they had been listening, both to the reports of what Jesus was doing and to the fact that He was passing by. Based on what they had heard, their faith was emboldened enough that they shouted to be heard above the crowd.

Second, why was the crowd yelling for them to be quiet? Were they selfishly vying for Jesus' attention, not wanting the blind men to be noticed? Were they doubtful that Jesus would or could heal the men? I'm not sure, but I wonder why the crowd didn't rally around these two men.

And third, they were not going to be quiet! The two blind men shouted LOUDER!

If you have a need and you're not heard the first time, do you get sullen and quiet or do you continue to speak up until you're heard?

This reminds me of a scripture that would inform what our response ought to be when we have a need.

66

"Ask and it will be given to you; seek and you will find;
knock and the door will be opened to you.
For everyone who asks receives; the one who seeks finds;
and to the one who knocks, the door will be opened."
—Matthew 7:7-8

When we study this scripture, the verbs suggest that one must *keep on asking, keep on seeking* and *keep on knocking* until the answer comes. So, I'm glad these two blind men shouted louder so they could be heard by Jesus and receive healing.

What about you? What do you need today? I encourage you to keep asking, seeking, and knocking until you have received your answer!

Day 32

When Given a Choice...

Exodus 13:17-15:18 / Matthew 21:23-46 / Psalm 26 / Proverbs 6:16-19

Do people ever make you so angry that you just want to slap them?! Okay, maybe that's a little dramatic, but you can't tell me you've never wished to do that... well, maybe you can. I do have some friends who are gentler of heart than myself!

Even if you don't want to physically hush someone up, I'm sure there have been times when you've wished a certain person would stop talking, arguing, etc. And why do we take the bait and continue an argument? We all know arguing doesn't provide any benefit.

My hubby Jeff is better at practicing that truth than I am. Jeffrey means "peacemaker" or "full of peace," and he is so good about choosing wisdom instead of irrational behavior, at least most of the time.

I used to be a terrible "hot head," but God has been working with me on that for a while. May I tell you a personal story before we get to what caused me to write this today?

When my oldest, Matthew, was little, maybe 18 months or so, I had a terrible temper, especially when I was driving. Unfortunately, I learned the behavior of yelling at other drivers from my dad (no disrespect intended!).

On this day, someone cut me off in traffic, and I yelled out, "You dumba**!!" No, my language is not always clean; sometimes it has "colors." I immediately heard the Holy Spirit rebuke me and say, "You will never talk that way again."

68

I became very aware of my little boy in the backseat, and I realized I was passing down a behavior that had been passed down to me. This was one of many situations where I was called to stand up and not allow the generational sins of my family to be passed along.

And that's part of why Still the Mom exists today because I am aware of a mandate to stand at the intersections and call out for truth. But before you can call out to others, you must take a hard look at your own shortcomings.

I wish I had lived my life up to this point more like Jesus did. He didn't argue when people were ignorant. Instead, He asked good questions, making them think and decide for themselves. He didn't try to convince anyone of anything; He simply lived and taught truth.

What about you? Do you argue, or do you live truth? I'm working hard to exemplify the latter. I'm not there yet, but that is my path!

Day 33

The Lord is My Fortress

Exodus 15:19-17:7 / Matthew 22:1-33 / Psalm 27:1-6 / Proverbs 6:20-26

I want to teach you a little bit today; meaning, let's dig a little deeper into a verse that I love to read and quote from Psalm 27:1.

"The LORD is my light and my salvation –
so why should I be afraid? The LORD is my fortress,
protecting me from danger, so why should I tremble?"

First, raise your hand if you want to be fearless. Don't you often wish you were genuinely afraid of nothing? I do! If I were fearless, what might I have done or be prepared to do with my life? That's a great question to consider all by itself!

Let's look deeper at Psalm 27:1.

"The LORD is my light and my salvation" – whatever the words "light" and "salvation" mean, they evidently remove fear, so let's find out their meaning.

"Light" is defined as "light of day," which to me means something by which I'm able to clearly see. Or said another way, the LORD allows me to clearly see.

"Salvation" is defined as "my rescue, safety, and victory."

How many of us are looking for a "hero" to rescue us? Jesus Christ rescued us from the penalty of sin when He went to the cross.

"Why should I be afraid?" Fear causes us to hesitate or stop when we should be moving forward. But if we have the LORD as our light so we can see, and as our safety to protect us, we should not fear if we're listening to Him and doing what He says! I promise it will be an adventure.

"The LORD is my fortress, protecting me from danger." "Fortress" is defined as "a place of safety, or a harbor." When I think of a fortress, I think of the medieval castles with moats, bridges and ramparts around the top which protected those inside from attack. The LORD is that kind of protection for those who are His.

"Why should I tremble?" This verse is saying the same thing twice, but the picture is a little different. If I'm trembling, I'm likely not moving anywhere; my feet are probably stuck in place. I can't even run from trouble. But if I know the LORD is protecting me, what might I do instead of standing and trembling?

I might either run from danger, or I may choose to stand and fight. Remember, fighting for the Jesus follower is done in prayer and worship.

Envision yourself as protected by God and able to see the path ahead. What were you afraid to do before that you're now willing to be brave about?

For me, it's pushing forward with allowing myself to walk in my calling as a spiritual mom. It's me being willing to share my life and my story, even knowing that some will receive, some will ignore, and some will reject my message. But God has told me to move forward, and He has given me the plan, so forward I will go!

Will you do the same with me?

Day 34

We Are All Equal

Exodus 17:8-19:15 / Matthew 22:34-23:12
Psalm 27:7-14 / Proverbs 6:27-35

Moses was wearing himself out trying to take care of every situation that came up with the people God had given him to lead. What he failed to realize was, he did not have to stand alone in leading them. It wasn't until his father-in-law Jethro saw what he was doing – working from morning until evening – that Jethro advised Moses to appoint other leaders to help with smaller matters, leaving Moses to decide larger matters and meet with God.

And this has been an oversight within the body of Christ, both from the perspective of the leaders and from the perspective of those within the body. What is being overlooked in the church? That the one man or woman in the pulpit, or even the small group of appointed leaders must bear the burden for the whole body. I don't believe God intended the church to operate this way.

Ephesians 4 says the called ministries of apostle, prophet, evangelist, pastor, and teacher are meant to equip and activate the rest of the body to do the work. That means everyone has work to do. Everyone is expected to learn, grow, mature, and serve. But sadly, many groups of believers are plagued with the few doing most of the work while the many sit and watch.

In Matthew 23:8 Jesus said, "All of you are equal as brothers and sisters." The context is that of the religious leaders taking pride in their position and prominence within the community. But Jesus is saying that no matter our gifts, calling or talents, we are all equal in His eyes!

That's what we are seeking to do in the church that meets in our home – equip everyone to know and understand their gift and position within the body, then activate them to operate there. It's such a joy, too – seeing each one take ownership within the community of believers. There's no fear of competition or stepping on another's toes; there is plenty of space for everyone to operate in the way God designed her or him.

Now that we're meeting this way, I'm finding that this type of fellowship has been hidden as a dream in my heart for years! I feel so blessed to be part of what God is doing at Bethesda Springs House of Mercy and Grace. If you don't have a church home, and you're in the Knoxville area, you're always welcome to visit!

Day 35

We Are Image Bearers

Exodus 19:16-21:21 / Matthew 23:13-39 / Psalm 28 / Proverbs 7:1-5

Reading in Exodus, we see the first instance of the Lord giving His people the Law or ten commandments. Most of them are very straight forward and easy to understand. Here are two of the commandments.

"You must not have any other God but Me. You must not make any image and worship it." (Exodus 20:3-5 paraphrased)

While each of these could use a little explanation, today I want to focus on the third commandment. What did God mean when He said we must not "misuse His Name," or "take His Name in vain?" Exodus 20:7

Here in the south, we think that means don't cuss using God's Name, and while I totally agree with that, there is a deeper meaning we find when we study a little further.

If I "take someone's name," I have become part of them. For example, when Jeff and I got married, I changed my last name from Wheeler to Kear; I took Jeff's name.

How do I know that's at least part of what is meant here? Listen to the definition of "take." Take is defined as "to lift up, bear, or carry." When I bear someone's name, it is part of my identity and title. When I was born, I became a Wheeler; I then bore my father's family name. When I was born again, born from Heaven, I took my Father's Name. I am now an image bearer and a representative of His.

What does it mean to carry His Name in vain? "Vain" is defined as "emptiness, nothingness, emptiness of speech, lying."

74

To me, this would mean I am misrepresenting the true nature and character of my Father in Heaven, either by my speech or my actions. I cannot call myself an image bearer of Christ if my speech and actions show Him to be someone other than who He really is.

That seems like a heavy burden; to bear a proper image of Christ. And it is; however, through the power of Holy Spirit, and with a heart willing to be molded to His will and purpose, I can grow in my ability to carry His name well.

One of my spiritual daughters, Jamie, used to say to me, "Momma Maria, I didn't shame the family name." She understood that she was representing our family when she was out and about because we were associated or connected with one another. When they saw her, they knew she was part of our family.

Are we shaming the family Name of Christ? Sometimes it's imperative to look at our thoughts and actions to see what others may be seeing in us.

I encourage you to be an image bearer worthy of the Name!

Day 36

The Lord Gives Strength and Peace

Exodus 21:22-23:13 / Matthew 24:1-28
Psalm 29 / Proverbs 7:6-23

Today I'm encouraged by two sentences in Psalm 29:11.

"The LORD gives His people strength.
The LORD blesses them with peace."

Strength and peace are something many of us need right about now! I know I need an increase in both, not from a natural perspective, but from the perspective of Heaven.

I just got off the phone with a friend, and we were talking about current world events. My answer to all that I'm seeing is, I want Heaven's perspective. I want to align myself with God's heart and His agenda. What other option is there?

If the Lord is giving me strength, He is giving me strength physically, materially, personally, socially, and politically. Yes, please! I receive that!

If He is giving me peace, He is giving me completeness, welfare, safety, soundness in body, health, prosperity, quiet, contentment, friendship with people and Himself, peace from war... those are such rich meanings and beautiful promises!

I was talking to another friend yesterday who is having a hard time understanding the chaos all around us, unanswered prayers, and God's involvement with His people. All I knew to tell her was that our perspective must be that of looking to God for Who He is. We must trust His character and His nature when we don't understand what's happening around us.

A lot of people are feeling uncertain, and I totally understand that. I feel that way also when I look at natural circumstances, but when I choose to look into the eyes of Jesus, I see that strength and peace I need.

Will you look into His eyes with me?

Day 37

People Get Ready

Exodus 23:14-25:40 / Matthew 24:29-51 / Psalm 30 / Proverbs 7:24-27

Reading Matthew reminds me of a song I used to love so much! It's called "People Get Ready" by Crystal Lewis. It speaks about a message that I've waited for the fulfillment of all my life – the return of Jesus Christ to gather His people to Himself. Here are some of the lyrics:

> "Lord, I'm ready now.
> I'm waiting for your triumphant return.
>
> People get ready . . .
> Soon we'll be going home."

Larry Norman wrote a similar song in 1969 called "I Wish We'd All Been Ready." I will allow you to search those lyrics and perhaps a video online. Now, that's a throwback!

Even typing those words now, and listening to these songs from years ago, causes such a fire of love to burn in my heart that I want to jump out of my skin and see His face today! I can't adequately describe the longing I feel to finally see face to face the One who created me. To know Him as He knows me.

But not everyone will be prepared to see Him. When I was a child there was a fireman who attended our small church where my dad was pastor. Every year we had to watch these movies that scared

78

us to death! End times, doom and gloom, or fiery hellish scenes. I grew up terrified of hell and was so full of fear.

But as I've studied this passage in Matthew more, I've come to realize that we were focusing on the wrong part of the story. Yes, there are those who will hear and turn away, and for that my heart is broken. But what about those who hear, believe and receive!

We will be caught up in the air to meet our returning King. It will be a day of great celebration. Why weren't there movies that focused more on that aspect? Maybe they wouldn't have sold as many tickets or reels.

Most stories have a comparison of good and evil, and for some reason we humans are drawn to the dark part of the story, but I believe we should switch that around in our brains. There is a loving Savior and Lord coming to be with us. Then He will create for us a new heaven and a new earth where we will live with Him forever.

We will receive love and joy and peace all because we believed and received. We did nothing to earn our salvation and once in heaven we will do nothing to remain in His presence. We will remain because He will remain, always. That's where I want my focus to be. This is what I choose to ponder.

Do you feel that same longing of heart? If not, all you must do is tell Him, "I want that!" He'll meet you right where you are.

Day 38

Do You Have Oil?

Exodus 26-27 / Matthew 25:1-30 / Psalm 31:1-8 / Proverbs 8:1-11

> "Aaron and his sons must keep the lamps burning
> in the Lord's presence all night."
> —Exodus 27:21b

In comparison, we have the parable of the ten bridesmaids or the ten virgins. All ten have lamps and all ten have oil in their lamps, but five of the bridesmaids have extra oil.

How can one keep a lamp burning if there is no oil?

It's true that we don't use lamps with oil any longer as they are a thing of the past, but the parallel is that of making sure we are filled with the Holy Spirit and that we are always prepared for the coming of Christ.

There is one ultimate preparation and that is our salvation; either we are His, or we are not. There are some who think they are His, but their lifestyle appears to be one other than someone who is in love with the ways and person of Jesus Christ. In other words, we can't only look like Christians outwardly, we must be genuine followers of Christ inwardly.

Maybe the five virgins who had oil were nice, religious "church goers" who looked good on the outside. Maybe they did good deeds, living a clean moral lifestyle. And that's not wrong to do, but good deeds don't reconcile us to God.

Jesus said in John 14:6, "I am the way and the truth and the life. No one comes to the Father except through me."

80

And that's the difference between the two groups of virgins. One may have been attempting Christianity from the perspective of living a good, moral life while the other understood that there is only one way to be reconciled to the Father, and that is through Jesus Christ the Son.

That is why the first five had extra oil; they had the Holy Spirit within them, and they were daily being filled and living in a way that pleased God. And we can't please God apart from His Spirit helping us live by faith.

Which bridesmaid are you? Do you have an empty lamp, or a full one? The time is drawing near for the return of Jesus Christ to take His people home. Make sure you're ready. We must keep our lamps burning with the Lord's presence all night!

Day 39

Common Grace

Exodus 28 / Matthew 25:31-26:13 / Psalm 31:9-18 / Proverbs 8:12-13

There are so many valuable nuggets of truth and wisdom in Proverbs. I could likely spend the entire year just in Proverbs and build a whole devotional series. Today, the verse that grabs my attention is this one:

"All who fear the Lord will hate evil. Therefore, I hate pride and arrogance, corruption, and perverse speech." Proverbs 8:13

"All who fear the Lord will hate evil." First, what is evil, and second, are we even aware of it? Finally, do we as followers of Jesus Christ sincerely hate evil?

And I have more questions. How do I hate evil, while loving people? How do I love people while not compromising toward sin? It's not possible for me to fully explore this topic in one short entry (already my mind is going 100 different directions), but let's see if we can pull a few truths out to process.

What does it mean to fear the Lord? Some might think this means I'm afraid of or hiding from Him. That's not what it means unless you're His enemy. Fear is defined as "terror, respect, reverence."

And though we probably have a good idea, what is evil? Evil is defined as "giving pain or misery, hurtful, ethically wicked in thoughts or actions, injury". To have respect and reverence for God means we will hate evil.

There's another verse in Isaiah 5:20 that says, "Woe to those who call evil good and good evil, who replace darkness with light and

82

light with darkness, who replace bitter with sweet and sweet with bitter."

I was reading yesterday about common grace, and I think it will help inform today's discussion. Common grace as defined in Lance Wallnau's book *God's Chaos Candidate* is "the grace that comes upon all, Christian and non-Christian, to help us affirm the good and resist the bad... the hidden hand of God that works to promote justice and order in a world where selfishness could produce societal collapse."

Every person is created by God, and we all have common grace on our lives. Some live with this grace in view, and some ignore it, preferring to call evil good and good evil.

We talked a few days ago about being a good, moral person. Common grace will allow one to be good and moral.

The thing that sets believers apart from the "common grace," good moral person is the one who has received God's saving grace of salvation.

I believe it is God's saving grace that allows us to fear God and truly hate evil. But to hate evil, we must awaken ourselves to its existence. And once we realize it exists, we must as followers of Jesus Christ stand against it.

A lot more could be said, but I'll stop here for now. One exhortation before you leave - please awaken to and stand against evil in our day. The world needs the justice of the Lord through the Church! What can you do to awaken and stand? Pray.

Day 40

Betrayal and Abandonment

Exodus 29:1-30:10 / Matthew 26:14-46
Psalm 31:19-24 / Proverbs 8:14-26

Betrayal and abandonment – Jesus suffered that and much more, including a brutal death on a cross. Have you ever put yourself in His place and tried to imagine both the physical and emotional pain? I can't even imagine. Yes, I know He was God, but His flesh would have felt every pain.

That's why when I suffer anything, I try to put things in perspective. I don't always succeed, but I try! And I suffered years of physical pain (more details as I share my story) as well as betrayal and abandonment. Which was worse? That's hard to say, but I think being betrayed and abandoned may have been worse because it seems harder to escape.

Jesus knew what was coming. He knew Judas would betray Him, and He knew Peter and the other disciples, men who had been his closest companions for three years, would abandon Him. His perspective on the whole story is the amazing part that we can learn from.

He forgave every person who hurt Him. He understood men's weaknesses. He had compassion. Do we?

Honestly, I'd rather get even. I'd rather see the other person suffer, until I realize that this attitude holds me as a prisoner. So, it is for my sake I must forgive and embrace the healing of my heart.

When we were part of a local church, before we started our home church in July of 2020, we attended and led something called

Freedom Groups. Freedom groups are powerful, and if you've never attended one, I highly recommend you do so!

One of the things the Freedom lessons teach is forgiveness and the concept that choosing not to forgive is akin to lighting yourself on fire and hoping the other person dies.

I know that's a graphic picture, but it's true. We forgive, not for the sake of the other person, but for our own sake. Bitterness and unforgiveness eat away at our own souls (and may also cause physical disease – yes, this is biblical!)

Who have you not forgiven? I encourage you to pray and do so right now. I'm serious. I wouldn't let another second go by holding onto unforgiveness. Please forgive – even if you must forgive the same person repeatedly until you feel released from the burden. Your physical and emotional health are worth the exercise.

So, part of working through betrayal and abandonment is to forgive those who hurt you. That is simple to say, but it's harder to walk out. However, the benefits will be massive toward healing your heart and the wounds in your soul.

Day 41

Unexpected Visitations

Exodus 30:11-31:18 / Matthew 26:47-68
Psalm 32 / Proverbs 8:27-32

Does it hurt anyone else's heart to the very core when reading about the way Jesus was treated when He was arrested? They brought clubs and swords to arrest a man who loved peace and loved people, healing and feeding them. Never mind the false accusations the religious leaders had against Him. What did they think He was going to do to them that they had to bring weapons?

I guess that's what deception looks like. The promised Messiah, God's own Son that they were all waiting for according to all the Old Testament prophecies, arrived in their lifetime, but because He didn't arrive according to their expectations, they missed a huge blessing.

If I had been alive, what side would I have been on? The side of the blind religious leaders? The scared disciples?

How often have we missed an opportunity from the Lord because a person or situation showed up in an unexpected "package"? Maybe that's why I like to look for the unexpected.

As of this writing, tomorrow is one month since our daughter lost her beloved fiancé Bradley, and I still believe we were visited by an angel in disguise in our time with him. I can't fully explain it – I just don't have the words or the understanding, but I know he impacted our family in eternal ways. And I believe we did the same for him.

When your life is interrupted and you feel you have been brought closer to Heaven, don't miss the opportunity to turn around and thank God for what He has done! I'm thankful every day for

86

God having brought Bradley into our lives, even though the time was way too short.

I'm anxious to get to Heaven one day and find out exactly what God intended. "But for now, I marvel at His saving grace and I'm full of praise once again" (a line from the song "Once Again" by Matt Redman).

The next time someone comes into your life, stop, and ask God what He intends. To not do so may cost you an incredible blessing and life-altering experience.

I'm so glad I listened.

Day 42

God is Near

Exodus 32-33 / Matthew 26:69-27:14
Psalm 33:1-11 / Proverbs 8:33-36

Moses said this to the Lord:

"If you don't personally go with us, don't make us leave this place . . .
for Your presence among us sets Your people and me
apart from all other people on the earth."
—Exodus 33:15

Why was God saying He would no longer go with His people? It was because of their sin of idolatry. God hates sin.

Sometimes we forget that God is both merciful and just. It is because of His justice that the penalty for our sin must be paid. But in His mercy, God sent Jesus Christ to pay that penalty by His death on the cross. Sin demanded payment, and God loved us enough to make the ultimate payment with His Son's life.

I won't pretend to fully understand God's character and nature. After all, though I'm a supernatural being having a natural experience, I still wrestle between my human and my spiritual mind.

But I do know this: I don't want to go anywhere in my life without God's presence. I need Him for all things. I need His wisdom and love, His justice and mercy, His forgiveness and strength.

In the Old Testament, before Jesus Christ came and before He sent the Holy Spirit to live inside us as His temples, the Spirit of God did leave people. That's hard for me to fathom, especially since God's

88

Spirit has lived inside me since childhood! I can't imagine what it would be like not to have Him nearby.

Is life still hard at times? Yes. Do I still feel alone, sad, angry, frustrated and confused at times? Yes, but the truth is, I'm never alone.

I've said many times that I don't comprehend how anyone could walk through life's difficulties without God's Spirit and presence. I'm thankful I'll never have to know that feeling again.

Day 43

We will see Him as He truly is

Exodus 34:1-35:9 / Matthew 27:15-31
Psalm 33:12-22 / Proverbs 9:1-6

As a follower and lover of Jesus Christ, one of my main goals has been to know Him; to understand His character, nature, and ways. Even after all this time, I can't pretend to fully understand God. Considering my unending pursuit of wanting to know Him more, there is a verse in 1 John 3:2 that is so exciting.

"Beloved, we are God's children right now; however, it is not yet apparent what we will become. But we do know that when it is finally made visible, we will be just like Him, for we will see Him as He truly is."

Do you see that end phrase? "We will see Him as He truly is." That means we will fully know God even as we are fully known by Him now. What an exciting day that will be!

But for now, we see only in part, and we understand only as far as our humanity can comprehend what Holy Spirit is revealing to us about God. That's why I love Exodus 34:6-7 because it is revealing God's nature.

"The Lord, the Lord, a God merciful and gracious, slow to anger, and abounding in steadfast love and faithfulness, keeping steadfast love for thousands, forgiving iniquity and transgression and sin, but who will by no means clear the guilty, visiting the iniquity of the fathers on the children and the children's children, to the third and the fourth generation."

Remember we talked yesterday about God being both merciful

90

and just. He is loving, but He must also bring judgment. We all love to remember his mercy and love, but it is so hard to fathom his justice and judgment. However, mercy and love would have no meaning when not balanced with justice and judgment.

In the earth there are both those who are righteous and those who are unrighteous, and in some ways, both receive from God's grace – remember the common grace spoken of a few days ago? However, there comes a time when we must be found in Christ to remain in His love and mercy.

May you be found in Christ today!

Day 44

Bless the Lord at all Times

Exodus 35:10-36:38 / Matthew 27:32-66
Psalm 34:1-19 / Proverbs 9:7-8

"I will bless the Lord at all times; His praise shall continually
be in my mouth. My soul will make its boast in the Lord;
the humble will hear it and rejoice. Exalt the Lord with me,
and let's exalt His name together."
—Psalm 34:1-3

Today's reading from Psalm 34 is so empowering and encouraging! When I read the first 3 verses, I saw a pattern of "I, they, we;" here's what I mean by that.

I must choose to bless (kneel, worship) the Lord at every moment in my life. I do this for myself and to honor my Savior. When I choose to bless the Lord, others will hear my praise, and it will give them courage! As I see that they are also encouraged, I will invite them to bless the Lord with me, and now we have a gathering of those who are blessing the Lord.

Our faith and courage are first for us, then for others. I don't live my life in a vacuum; my life is laid out for all to see. This reminds me of a scripture in 2 Corinthians 3:1-3 that talks about our lives being a letter that all people may read. If that's true, what are others "reading" in your life?

As usual, this is not a call for perfection, but it is an exhortation for submission to the purpose and will of Jesus Christ, both for

92

your sake and the sake of those watching – and, believe me, they are watching.

I became aware that others were watching my life several years ago. The fact that others were taking notice of my actions and attitudes both terrified me and made me want to live my life in a way to honor God. I also wanted to be sure I was being a good example so others would also grow in their relationship with Jesus Christ.

Bless the Lord today, and encourage others to do the same, then we'll all be stronger!

Day 45

An Earthquake, an Angel, and a Message

Exodus 37-38 / Matthew 28 / Psalm 34:11-22 / Proverbs 9:9-10

"They were very frightened but also filled with great joy ..."
—Matthew 28:8.

Something about this statement grabbed my attention as I read today's passage in Matthew. Mary Magdalene and "the other Mary" had arrived at Jesus's tomb just in time for an earthquake, an angel, and a message. Can you imagine having been there to see this history-altering event?

This is the 2nd earthquake within a three-day span; one at Jesus's death and now one at His resurrection. I wonder how many put two and two together and figured out a huge event had occurred?

Have you ever seen an angel? I have not, but I know people who have, and I've heard they are very imposing. So, it makes sense the women would have been frightened. I'm sure they were trying to sort through what they were hearing, feeling, and seeing.

Then the message came, and it was the message that brought clarity to the shaking and the supernatural appearance of the angel. And it is the Word of God that brings revelation and understanding to every situation in our lives.

Today in our church gathering we talked about this verse in Hebrews 4:12 – "For the word of God is alive and active. Sharper than any double-edged sword, it penetrates even to dividing soul and spirit, joints, and marrow; it judges the thoughts and attitudes of the heart."

94

Some think the Bible is not relevant in our lives, but I disagree because the above verse proves that God's Word brings us discernment for every situation.

So, the next time you sense a shaking, or you see something that doesn't make sense, look to the Bible for clarity and understanding.

Day 46

God, My Righteous Judge

Exodus 39-40 / Mark 1:1-28 / Psalm 35:1-16 / Proverbs 9:11-12

We've all had arguments, disagreements, etc. with others. Some were able to be resolved and some were not. Have you ever had such a sharp disagreement that it was necessary to part ways? Of course, in those circumstances it's imperative we forgive, but the truth is we may or may not be reconciled to that person or persons.

We faced such a circumstance a few years ago, and though it was painful and there was a lot of misunderstanding, the Lord was clear. He told us, "Allow them to say whatever they'd like; do not defend yourselves. Remember that vengeance is mine."

It is so hard to keep quiet, remove yourself completely from a situation having no contact, and allow God to do what He knows is best, but that is exactly what we did. And today, we've moved on, and we're more blessed and healthier than we've been in many years, thanks be to God!

So, when I read Psalm 35:1, I was reminded again that it is the Lord who is our defender.

> "O LORD oppose those who oppose me.
> Fight those who fight against me."

In the New American Standard Bible, the word "oppose" is "contend" and part of that is a legal term meaning "to conduct a case or legal suit." In essence, I'm asking the Lord to open His courtroom, present the evidence on my behalf and render a verdict.

96

The word "fight" implies that we are to go to battle, and this also makes me think of a court battle. If God is my righteous Judge (and He is!), I am counting on Him to stand and speak on my behalf. That means I don't always have to defend myself, because He is going to step in and do so! That is a huge comfort to me because people don't always want to listen to reason.

If you're facing a situation, ask God what your response should be. Do you speak up, or do you allow God to defend you? Whichever is true, please know that God is on your side. And He is also always on the side of truth.

Day 47

Don't Forget the Salt

Leviticus 1-3 / Mark 1:29-2:12 / Psalm 35:17-28 / Proverbs 9:13-18

> "Season all your grain offerings with salt to remind you
> of God's eternal covenant. Never forget to add salt
> to your grain offerings."
> —Leviticus 2:13

"Everyone will pass through the fire and every sacrifice will be seasoned with salt." Mark 9:49 (not part of today's reading).

The sacrifices of the Old Testament have been done away with because Jesus Christ is our one perfect sacrifice. We who are in covenant with Him through His blood are now called to offer our lives as a sacrifice of worship. Romans 12:1

When God commanded the Old Testament sacrifices to be salted as they were offered, it was said that the aroma pleased Him. Mark 9:49 tells us that every sacrifice will be seasoned with salt. For us today, that means as we go through troubles and sorrows choosing to praise Him, our lives will be "salted" to be a beautiful fragrance for Him.

There is further meaning to be found in Mark 9 regarding our fiery trials, sacrifice, and salt. Some Greek texts translate the meaning of verse 9 as "everyone will be salted with fire." If you've lived any length of time as a Christian, you know that trials are part of our journey. As a matter of fact, Jesus promised we would have hard times.

"And everything I've taught you is so that the peace which is in Me will be in you and will give you great confidence as you rest in Me. For in this unbelieving world, you will experience trouble

98

and sorrows, but you must be courageous, for I have conquered the world." John 16:33

The test is in how we respond during hard times. Do we become angry and difficult to live with, or do we cling more tightly to our faith and remain faithful? Since trials are going to come, we would do well to prepare ourselves for them by understanding what trials bring into our lives.

James 1:2-4 tells us, "That when our faith is tested it stirs up in you the power of endurance ... endurance ... will release perfection into every part of your being until there is nothing missing and nothing lacking" (The Passion Translation.)

When you're faced with your next "salty trial," keep in mind that you are gaining endurance and perfection as a result. I pray that you face your trials with tenacity and hope!

Day 48

Find the Hidden Beauty

Leviticus 4-5 / Mark 2:13-3:6 / Psalm 36 / Proverbs 10:1-2

Anyone who knows me well knows that my family and I love people as they are. We don't just say that; we believe and practice loving people no matter where they are in life. We don't try to fix them or change them; we love them and trust God to do the fixing and changing. For that reason, I love two portions from today's reading.

In Mark 2:15-17 Jesus is invited to the house of a tax collector, a hated person in Jewish society, and He is criticized by the Pharisees for doing so. His response is that healthy people don't need a doctor – sick people do.

Jesus knew where He was going to be received and He understood the hearts of those who knew their need for Him.

I also love verses 7-8 in Psalm 26. "All humanity finds shelter in the shadow of your wings. You feed them from the abundance of your own house, letting them drink from your river of delights."

Only a generous, loving God allows others to find shelter with Him. Only a discerning man or woman will feed someone from his abundance.

It's easy to see the faults of others while overlooking our own. I guess that's human nature – to look outside of us at the faults instead of looking within. But what if we chose to look within ourselves first? If we did, I think we would be more concerned with changing ourselves instead of others, trusting that others are able to look within to find what needs adjustment.

Most of us are painfully aware of our shortcomings; we don't need others to remind us. I've heard it said that people grow more with positive reinforcement than they do with criticism. What if we looked for the positive in others and praised them for that? I believe it would cause them to rise to the occasion and work to amend the weak areas in their lives.

We have a saying at our house – it's easy to be Captain Obvious and point out the negative. What if we looked beyond the obvious to find the deep inner beauty in others?

Who can you find beauty in today? I bet you'll change that person's day and life!

Day 49

Don't Let the Fire Go Out

Leviticus 6:1-7:27 / Mark 3:7-30 / Psalm 37:1-11 /Proverbs 10:3-4

While reading the passage from Leviticus, there was a spark, and that led me to read the following additional passage.

Romans 12:11-21 "Never be lazy but work hard and serve the Lord enthusiastically. Rejoice in our confident hope. Be patient in trouble and keep on praying. When God's people are in need, be ready to help them. Always be eager to practice hospitality. Bless those who persecute you. Don't curse them; pray that God will bless them. Be happy with those who are happy, and weep with those who weep. Live in harmony with each other. Don't be too proud to enjoy the company of ordinary people. And don't think you know it all! Never pay back evil with more evil. Do things in such a way that everyone can see you are honorable. Do all that you can to live in peace with everyone. Dear friends, never take revenge. Leave that to the righteous anger of God. For the Scriptures say, 'I will take revenge; I will pay them back,' says the Lord. Instead, if your enemies are hungry, feed them. If they are thirsty, give them something to drink. In doing this, you will heap burning coals of shame on their heads. Don't let evil conquer you but conquer evil by doing good."

When I started reading the above passage of scripture, I couldn't simply stop with verse 11. In Leviticus, God warned the priests that the fire on the altar must never go out. That warning caused me to think about the fact that the fire of the Holy Spirit must never be allowed to be extinguished in our hearts.

102

I've loved Jesus since I was a child. I've had seasons when my heart was on fire for Him and seasons when my heart was indifferent, but in most seasons my heart has been aflame with passion for the One who loves my soul. Even as I write this, my heart is on fire with love for Jesus Christ.

I kept reading because I discovered that the fruit of that fire in our hearts are the things that follow in verses 12-21. There is so much beautiful and needed instruction in these verses, but there is also proof of what it looks like to be in Christ.

Do you ever wonder whether someone is sincerely a follower of Christ? These verses seem like a good test of whether we are following Him. I'm not saying we live this life perfectly, but we ought to strive to live in such a way that we would be convicted if tried in a court of law.

As you read the above verses, which concept stands out to you? For me it was "Don't be too proud to enjoy the company of ordinary people." But all the content is convicting to my heart.

Today I'll strive to be a friend to ordinary people. Tomorrow, I may focus on overcoming evil with good!

Day 50

God Laughs at His Enemies.
Why Shouldn't I?

Leviticus 7:28-9:6 / Mark 3:31-4:25 / Psalm 37:12-29 / Proverbs 10:5

How many of you get quickly irritated when someone "does you wrong"? In a general sense, I'm looking at two categories of people – those who notice the irritating things people do toward them and those who don't. I wish I were more like the second category. I want to talk about a third category.

What if those irritating things aren't pointed toward you at all? What if that person is simply self-focused and not aware of his or her bad behavior? While I can't tell you about the statistics on how often it's one or the other, I can tell you that we are too quickly bothered by a "something" that is more likely a "nothing". Not many people are the type who intentionally want to cause another person to become angry. Most are totally unaware.

Psalm 37:12 is speaking of those who are intentionally evil. "The wicked plot against the godly; they snarl at them in defiance."

If you know that someone is intentionally being evil, how do you respond to that? That's a loaded question, and I'm not saying I have a simple answer, but I can tell you how God feels about it!

Psalm 37:13 says, "But the Lord just laughs, for he sees their day of judgment coming."

God looks into the eternal future, seeing past the present evil that is intended. And this can apply both personally and on a larger and more general scale. How many of you have been angry because

104

it seems that people who are evil get away with everything? I know I have! It seems I try to live my life to please God and be kind to people while "she" is being completely selfish and mean and nothing bad ever happens to her!

I have two thoughts here. One is that we don't see the totality of her life. She likely has some terrible things happening or she wouldn't be so mean. The second is, we all reap what we're sowing – meaning, you get what you give. That is a law of nature. If you're being mean, you'll get "mean" back. If you're being kind, you'll get "kind" back. That said, we all have tough times.

The Lord laughing makes me think of a lady in scripture who also laughed.

> "She is clothed with strength and dignity,
> and she laughs without fear of the future."
> —Proverbs 31:25

The Hebrew word for laugh is the same in both passages and it means "to laugh in contempt or derision, to mock." Interesting, but how can one laugh during difficult times? It's only possible if you know the One who holds the future in His hands.

I've said this before – the circumstances may not change. You may continue to have trouble, but God is always good, even in the hard seasons.

Keep your eyes fixed on God and laugh at your enemies. Another way to "laugh" at your enemies is to pray and worship. I dare you to try it!

Day 51

Mercy Triumphs over Justice

Leviticus 9:7-10:20 / Mark 4:26-5:20 / Psalm 37:30-40 / Proverbs 10:6-7

Scripture is full of comparison and contrast. For example, we read about the wicked and the godly, evil and good, and clean and unclean. We see a lot of these type comparisons in the four Gospels, especially through the parables that Jesus taught.

Today there is both good and evil at work in the earth, and it's difficult and painful to look evil in the face. I've seen and heard things over the last few years that have rocked me. But still, I know that God is good.

There was a phrase in Leviticus 10 that caused me to stop and think, and it was followed by a sentence. The phrase is "And Aaron was silent", and the sentence is in verse 10 – "You must distinguish between what is sacred and what is common..."

First, why was Aaron silent? His sons had just been consumed by the fire of God for not following His prescribed protocols in the Tabernacle. I realize this seems harsh to some; it's hard to fathom myself. But I think we forget, as I spoke of a few days ago, that God is both loving and just. If He tells us to do things a certain way, to go contrary to that will bring a consequence of some kind.

Aaron was silent, because he understood what had happened: the justice of God had been meted out.

That brings me to the sentence where we are told to distinguish between what is sacred and what is common. First, let me say that if we're in Christ, we have become sacred, holy, and set apart because of

106

His sacrifice on the cross. And it is from our position of holiness that we may judge between good and evil.

There is so much happening in our nation – evil is being called good and good is being called evil. And don't think God doesn't notice what's happening. He does. It is because of His great love that we are not consumed. Yet, evil will be judged.

Sometimes we are concerned that evil goes unpunished, but it does not. Again, God sees. Justice is something I have prayed for a lot lately. Sometimes, it's the only word I can get out of my mouth because my heart is so heavy. And I know God is bringing justice.

Some may think this post is sobering, and it is. But remember that God's love means little to us without the balance of His justice. If we experienced only love, justice would have no weight. And if we experienced only justice, love would have no weight.

Lord, in Your wrath, remember mercy. Habakkuk 3:2

Day 52

Exchange Fear for Faith

Leviticus 11-12 / Mark 5:21-43 / Psalm 38 / Proverbs 10:8-9

There is a lot happening in Mark 5, but the phrase that caught my attention today is something Jesus spoke to Jairus upon hearing the news that his daughter had died. Jesus said (in the NASB), "Do not be afraid any longer, only believe."

For Jesus to tell Jairus not to be afraid any longer, must mean that Jairus was coming in fear, as I can imagine one would if his daughter was dying. I can certainly tell you I would also have been afraid. But Jesus is asking Jairus to make an exchange.

Exchange fear for faith.

The word "believe" means "to be persuaded of, to think to be true, to place confidence in."

In that moment, as Jairus looked into Jesus's eyes, I bet he saw something that gave him courage, that gave him hope.

How many times have you chosen to look into Jesus's eyes when all your hope is gone? When fear threatens to overwhelm you? And when you looked, what did you find? Peace? Answered prayer? Love?

You probably saw all of that and so much more. I love these words. Jesus knew what Jairus did not – a miracle was coming! Jesus saw beyond the natural world into the supernatural world, where it had been determined that this young girl's life was far from over. She was going to live!

In this account we find an important reminder for ourselves – do not look at what you see in the natural. Instead, look to Jesus to find out what He wants to do in your situation. No matter how

108

difficult or hopeless things may seem, Jesus has a plan, and He is not only willing to share that plan with you, but also to come to you with an answer.

What are you facing? Where will you look today?

Day 53

Do You Believe?

Leviticus 13 / Mark 6:1-29 / Psalm 39 / Proverbs 10:10

"Jesus was amazed at their unbelief."
—Mark 6:6

Each day is a little different as I read the Bible; sometimes a section catches my eye and sometimes just one phrase does. Today, the above phrase caught my attention. Jesus is back in His hometown of Nazareth, doing what He always does now – meeting in the Synagogue to teach on the Sabbath, and healing all those the Father sends.

But today is different. Jesus has seen crowds following Him everywhere He goes, all wanting to be near Him so they can hear what He has to say, but also so they can receive the healing He carries. But in his hometown, the people are deeply offended and refuse to believe Him.

Even though Jesus was God in human flesh, He must have known He would be rejected by His own hometown. And I bet it was hurtful to Him. It would have made me sad to be rejected by the people who knew me best – my own family and friends. Maybe this is part of why He was called a Man of sorrows.

Isaiah 53:3 says, "He was despised and rejected— a man of sorrows, acquainted with deepest grief. We turned our backs on him and looked the other way. He was despised, and we did not care."

He was amazed at their unbelief. The word amazed means "feeling or showing great surprise or wonder." Unbelief is defined as "incredulity or skepticism especially in matters of religious faith."

110

If Jesus were here now, teaching and performing miracles, would I believe Him? What if I told you He is here, in the form of His Remnant Church, and He is still speaking and performing miracles through His word and His people.

Do you believe?

Day 54

Fill Your Clay Jar with Fresh Water

Leviticus 14 / Mark 6:30-56 / Psalm 40:1-10 / Proverbs 10:11-12

"The words of the godly are a life-giving fountain."
—Proverbs 10:11a

In today's reading, there were several connected thoughts. In Mark we saw where crowds followed Jesus everywhere He went because they were hungry spiritually, but also because they were hungry physically. Jesus "fed" both needs.

As we read, we also see that the crowds were relentless. The need was so large and never-ending that Jesus and His disciples found it difficult to find time to rest and refresh. Even when they tried to get in the boat and find a quiet place to rest, the people followed them.

Then in Psalm 40 the Psalmist is waiting patiently for the Lord to help him, and as always, the Lord turned to him and heard his cry. Our Heavenly Father is always there. He never gets tired of answering our prayers and taking care of our needs. His words do bring us life.

And just as Jesus taught, we are also to bring words of life to those around us. We are the godly spoken of in Proverbs and when we speak the words God gives, they produce life in others.

But what if you find yourself inundated with needs as Jesus did? If Jesus, the Son of God, needed to rest and refresh by meeting with His Father, how much more do we need to do the same! I'm not saying we should ignore the needs around us, but I am saying we must be cautious concerning the potential to burn out.

112

If we're not spending time alone with God, filling up on His word and presence, both praying and listening to His voice, we will have no words of life to give. We may even find ourselves in danger of offering human wisdom which will not bring life to ourselves, let alone anyone else.

So, please be prepared to offer those life-giving words, but don't forget to fill the "jar" of your soul with His presence so that what you're pouring out for others is fresh water.

At one of our house church gatherings, as we were talking about our message for the morning, the Lord began speaking around the room about a section in 2 Corinthians 4 that says, "but we have this treasure in jars of clay, to show that the surpassing power belongs to God and not to us."

Let us not forget that the treasure we hold in our "jar" is God's Spirit, meant to be poured into us and out to others.

Day 55

If You Need a Friend...

Leviticus 15:1-16:28 / Mark 7:1-23
Psalm 40:11-17 / Proverbs 10:13-14

The Pharisees were always washing everything with water including their hands and their dishes. Why? They thought this made them clean, pure, and right before God. I'll admit that I like things to be clean. I may or may not be a little bit of a germaphobe. But if I had to choose between clean hands and a clean heart, I'd choose a clean heart.

Jesus said, "It's not what goes into your body that defiles you, you are defiled by what comes from your heart." Mark 7:15

How do we know what is in someone's heart? It comes right out of her mouth! Or it's shown in her actions, which I think speaks even louder than what is said. Some people show their true character right away, and with some it takes a little longer. But no one can pretend to be who they are not for long.

Are you truly kind? Are you truthful? Or do you live a double life? Do you cut and run the minute things get tough? I could ask a hundred more questions that would help determine who a person is at her core.

Don't get me wrong; we're all imperfect. However, we must decide if those we've chosen to walk with are the ones with whom we're willing to embrace the good, the bad and the ugly! And if you've found a group of people who want to do the same with you – embrace your good, bad, and ugly – you're rich indeed!

114

Everyone's relationships go through highs and lows, good times and bad. Remember, there are "safe" and "unsafe" people. And there is nothing wrong with discerning between the two and choosing to set your boundaries, spending the bulk of your time with "safe" people.

Some have been taught that we must accept all people, and to some degree I agree with that. I will give anyone a chance. But I will not allow everyone into my intimate inner circle space. That space is reserved for those who have proven to have the highest of character; those who have proven they have my back no matter what.

I am blessed to have an amazing group of family and friends who fit these criteria. As a matter of fact, I believe I'm rich in that area!

You've also heard it said that to have a friend, you must be a friend. A friend is defined as "one attached to another by affection or esteem. One that is not hostile. One that is of the same nation, party, or group. A favored companion."

I invite you today to look around you and evaluate the ones who are close. Are they safe? Are they truly friends? Do you need to make any changes? Or do you simply need to thank God for the blessings He's given?

Day 56

God Causes the Growth

Leviticus 16:29-18:30 / Mark 7:24-8:10 / Psalm 41 / Proverbs 10:15-16

If we had lived in Jesus's day, we may have thought Him very strange. In Mark there is a man who cannot hear or speak and what does Jesus do? He takes him away from the crowd so they can be alone, then he sticks His fingers in the man's ear and spits on his fingers, touching the man's tongue. Okay...

This is not the only instance where Jesus healed someone using an unusual method. And while I can't explain why Jesus chose to heal in these odd ways, I can tell you that His heart of compassion brought healing to everyone He encountered.

What about us? In my upcoming book titled "Word of the Week", on the entry titled "Empathy", I talk about the meaning of compassion. Compassion is defined as "when we are moved into action to alleviate the suffering of another."

We're sometimes good at having compassion and taking action to meet physical needs, but what about spiritual needs? What about when someone has a need for physical healing? What about those who are oppressed by the devil?

Jesus cast out many demons from people; we should be prepared to do the same. But sometimes we shy away from praying for people, both for healing and for the release of demonic influence. Why? I'm sure there are many reasons.

Maybe we doubt our ability to be effective. Maybe we're fearful we'll see no results. That doesn't mean we shouldn't pray!

I'm reminded of a scripture in 1 Corinthians 3:7 NASB that

116

says, "So then neither the one who plants nor the one who waters is anything, but God who causes the growth."

Our responsibility is to pray; God's responsibility is to answer, heal and deliver. That doesn't mean we approach the situation unprepared. We must prepare with prayer, forgiveness, and sometimes fasting. It is my opinion that we should always pray when faced with a situation that is God's to resolve.

Our resources will be of great value, but God's resources are of eternal value. So, let's offer God's resources at every opportunity!

Day 57

Gain the World and Lose Your Soul?

Leviticus 19:1-20:21 / Mark 8:11-38 / Psalm 42 / Proverbs 10:17

Jesus said to Peter, "You are seeing things merely from a human
point of view, not from God's."
—Mark 8:33b

The concept of seeing things from Heaven's perspective is something I have been thinking about a lot, something the Lord has been pressing upon my heart daily. It is by no means an easy process to change one's thinking, but I know it's possible. After all, scripture tells us we must renew our minds. Romans 12:2

In the verses that follow in Mark chapter 8, there are some clues as to what actions may signify one who has Heaven's view. Here's what Jesus said about the subject.

"If any of you wants to be my follower, you must give up your own way, take up your cross, and follow me. If you try to hang on to your life, you will lose it. But if you give up your life for my sake and for the sake of the Good News, you will save it. And what do you benefit if you gain the whole world but lose your soul?" Mark 8:34-36

Once again, we've encountered the Upside-Down Kingdom of Heaven. If I want to follow Jesus, I must give up my own way. If I want to follow Him, I must take up my cross. By holding onto my life, I lose it. By giving up my life, I save it. Are you thoroughly confused?

If you are confused, I understand. It can be confusing because we've been taught in the western world to take care of number one, or ourselves. So, it makes no sense to give up our own way or to lose our

118

lives. But in God's view, we are giving up a way of human understanding, which is a limited picture, for His understanding. And He sees everything, the things that have been revealed to us and the things that are still hidden.

It's the hidden things of God's Kingdom which make the difference in how we choose to live our lives. While I'm trying to "gain the whole world", I'm losing my soul. While I'm looking at my life through the glasses of humanity, I'm losing God's perspective which would bring me true life, peace, and prosperity.

To understand this Upside-Down Kingdom, it takes a new perspective, as well as thinking and seeing according to Heaven's view. That is what I'm actively pursuing and attempting to gain – a vantage point of my life, and life around me, from God's perspective. And why wouldn't I want that? He sees what I can't see! I need His wisdom and direction.

What about you? Have you considered what it might be like to see your life and the lives of those around you from God's view? How might this change the way you approach your decisions and daily living?

Day 58

Our Prayer for Today

Leviticus 20:22-22:16 / Mark 9:1-29/ Psalm 43 / Proverbs 10:18

"Send out Your light and Your truth; let them guide me.
Let them lead me to Your holy mountain,
to the place where You live."
—Psalm 43:3

Here is Psalm 43:3 again with some key words defined.

"Send out (stretch out, extend) your light (everywhere diffused) and your truth (firm and stable peace, security, constant and perpetual favor of God, integrity, justice, and sincerity); let them guide me. (put on my original, straight path) Let them lead me to your holy mountain, to the place where you live."

Today's devotional thought is a simple heart cry and prayer. There is great power in praying scripture and this verse is a perfect example of doing that. Please read the verse above again and read it as a prayer and see if you notice the beauty and power of this practice.

As a follower of Christ, I want to be near Him. I want to hear His voice and know His ways. If He is walking in a direction, I want to follow. If He has changed course, I want to know so I can adapt.

I want to walk where He walks, hear what He hears and see what He sees. I desire to align my heart with His both because I love Him and because that is the safest space for me to inhabit.

120

Day 59

Make the Most of Each Moment

Leviticus 22:17-23:44 / Mark 9:30-10:12/ Psalm 44:1-8 / Proverbs 10:19

There are some verses in Mark that grabbed my heart – several really, but I don't have space to write about them all!

In one of our house church gatherings there was a tangible sense of God revealing Himself and His heart to us, so I'm processing today's scriptures from a place of having been visited by God's strong and loving presence.

"Jesus didn't want anyone to know he was there, for he wanted to spend more time with his disciples and teach them." Mark 9:30-31

There is so much emotion behind this statement. Jesus knew His crucifixion was near and that He wouldn't see His friends on earth much longer. I'm sure His heart ached due to the impending separation, and He wanted to spend as much time with them as possible!

What if we lived with this type of attitude toward those we love? What if I knew that I had just a few days left with my favorite people? Would I also want to hide away for some private time, making sure I expressed to them my most important thoughts? I know I would!

I remember when my daddy was in the hospital in September of 2016 before he passed to Heaven Oct 3. The Lord had already spoken to me that He was taking my daddy home, and I knew the time was short, so I spent every minute in his presence that I possibly could because I knew I would not see him this way again. The next time I see him we will both be in our Heavenly bodies. I wanted to squeeze all the sweetness out of our time together.

And don't you think God is that way with us? Don't you think He loves spending time with us? I know I love spending time with Him!

There is one more sentence that gives a side thought to what's on my heart. "You must have the qualities of salt among yourselves and live in peace with each other." Mark 9:50

I love that! Salt brings flavor and richness, and we are to bring flavor and richness to one another's lives! "Live in peace with each other." I think that's a beautiful command.

We don't know when it may be the final time we'll be with a person we love. I would hate to think we missed an opportunity to bless and show love. Missed opportunities do not have to happen, not if we're living life fully aware.

That's how I want to live! When I leave this earth, I want to know that I loved with all I had in me! What about you? Let's do it!!

Day 60

Words of Sterling Silver

Leviticus 24:1-25:46 / Mark 10:13-31/ Psalm 44:9-26 / Proverbs 10:20-21

> "The words of the godly are like sterling silver
> and the words of the godly encourage many."
> —Proverbs 10:20

The speech, or what comes out of their mouths, of those who are right with God is valuable. In other words, what the godly says has been carefully chosen and given out to others because it will produce value or carry weight in the lives of those who listen.

To me, the thought behind the action of speech is that the words were carefully pondered before spoken. There was no impulsive pouring out of words, but rather a well-thought-out dialogue with the specific intent of bringing life, health, and peace to the listener.

Have you ever met someone who seems to talk just to hear her own voice? They talk on and on and before long you realize you're no longer listening. That's why it's important to be one of few words, so that when you do have something to share, the value is immediately received and understood.

If the words of the godly are meant to encourage many, they must be God's words and not our own. Our own words may be nice, even kind, but God's words carry life in them. God's words carry the ability to bring healing in the soul, and to help us understand the meaning of what God intended for our lives.

So, before you speak, consider, pray and be certain what you're bringing will bless the ones listening. Does that mean we'll never have

124

a careless word? No. I'm sure we'll still have lots of those, but perhaps we'll find ourselves being more thoughtful. And I have a feeling we'll find our audience more enraptured.

Day 61

Jesus, Our Mighty Warrior

Leviticus 25:47-27:13 / Mark 10:32-52 / Psalm 45 / Proverbs 10:22

The Church has her eyes and heart divided into many spaces during this time. She is looking all around her for a savior – one who will deliver her from all her fears. It was interesting to note in Mark that the disciples who were walking closely with Jesus were in "awe", while those who were "following behind" were "overwhelmed with fear."

Our Father has graciously allowed us free will. We are free to look at, taste, touch, smell and hear whatever we choose. However, this is both a blessing and a curse. We must be discerning of what we partake.

Even when Jesus came into public view, many thought He was coming to free them from Roman rule. They didn't understand that He came to free them from the rule of sin, which is of more widespread effect.

Many of us look at the near, the small picture, our own little world. But God is looking at the big picture, at eternity. I'm not saying we should never see the trees, but we must not neglect the forest. The place upon which our eyes focus matters.

I'm sure you can see where this is going! We must have eyes for only One. That's why I love Psalm 45 that describes Jesus so beautifully. Verses 2-5 are breathtaking!

"You are the most handsome of all. Gracious words stream from your lips. God himself has blessed you forever. Put on your sword, O mighty warrior! You are so glorious, so majestic! In your majesty, ride out to victory, defending truth, humility, and justice. Go forth to perform awe-inspiring deeds! Your arrows are sharp, piercing your enemies' hearts. The nations fall beneath your feet."

If you are concerned about what's happening in our nation and world, reading the above passage will remind you of Who is in charge! Please remember that God is working behind the scenes to set up a Heavenly Kingdom that will not be destroyed. If you're in Christ, you're a part of that Kingdom, and no fear is permitted in His presence!

Let me encourage you today. Yes, the world looks a little scary. Yes, there are many different opinions regarding how things will play out. But there is nothing you can do about any of that (except stay in prayer). What you can do is focus on the Father – His heart, His purpose, His will. He is at work.

Ask Him to show you what He's doing so you can align with that. I promise it will bring you peace no matter what you see with your eyes or hear with your ears.

Day 62

A Stolen Donkey and a Revealed Messiah

Leviticus 27:14 – Numbers 1:54 / Mark 11:1-26
Psalm 46 / Proverbs 10:23

Somebody stole my donkey!! Y'all, I just couldn't help but laugh a little when reading Mark's account of Jesus telling His disciples to go steal a colt. No, He didn't actually tell them to steal anything, but to an onlooker it likely appeared that way.

He told them to go into a village where they would see a young donkey that had never been ridden. They were instructed to untie it and bring it back. And if someone asked what they were doing, they were to tell them, "The Lord needs it and will return it soon." Mark 11:3

Okay, moving on from the funny part, I had another thought. Since Holy Spirit speaks to all of us, is it possible that those who were being asked about the donkey knew that if someone came to them saying that the Lord needed the donkey, it was okay to allow that? From all my years of hearing God and noticing an agreement among brothers and sisters in Christ, I think this is highly likely.

So, as odd as it may have appeared to everyone involved, perhaps Holy Spirit had spoken to everyone, so no one was taken by surprise, and everyone was blessed in the giving and receiving of this little donkey.

Going further, I've wondered who told Jesus to get on the donkey and ride through the streets. I would guess it was at His Father's request. And beyond that, who prompted the people to spread garments and leafy branches for Jesus to ride upon? Again, I think Holy

128

Spirit was at work revealing the Messiah to those who were hearing and acting. And that's just what the spirit of prophecy is.

There is a part of Revelation 19:10 that says, "Worship only God. For the essence of prophecy is to give a clear witness for Jesus."

I believe prophecy was at work in this whole story in Mark 11 because Jesus was being revealed to everyone watching. And He is still being revealed today. I believe we can look for Him in all of life's circumstances, because He is always at work even when we don't see the evidence.

Day 63

With Joyful Shouts!

Numbers 2-3 / Mark 11:27-12:17/ Psalm 47 / Proverbs 10:24-25

In my opinion, praise is meant to be loud and full of joy, shouting, clapping of the hands, even dancing or jumping. I've done all these and there are times I just can't help myself because I'm so overcome with the goodness and beauty of God! Have you ever felt that way?

In reading Psalm 47, I get a sense of great joy and celebration! "Come everyone! Clap your hands! Shout to God with joyful praise!" (Psalm 47:1) I can feel the energy and I'm excited just reading the words.

But sometimes we're hesitant to praise in a demonstrative way because of what others may think. I get that. However, if we knew what our praise accomplishes in the Spirit, I believe we would crank it up louder!

What does our praise accomplish?

Praise allows us to see God as He is. Why? Because He inhabits our praise, and when His presence is near, He is revealing His character. In one of our home church gatherings there was a heavy awareness of God doing this. His presence was noticed and there was a deep revelation of His love and care.

Praise gives us proper perspective. If the songs we sing are doctrinally strong, we're learning about God and His kingdom and having our minds renewed. Is anyone interested in a sermon in song? Well, a properly written worship song will feed into the truth of Who God is.

Praise prepares the way for battle. In Numbers, it was the tribes of Judah, Issachar and Zebulun who led whenever the Israelites traveled to a new campsite. The name Judah means "praise".

In 2 Chronicles 20:21 it says, "After consulting the people, the king appointed singers to walk ahead of the army, singing to the Lord and praising him for his holy splendor. This is what they sang: 'Give thanks to the Lord; his faithful love endures forever!'"

Praise destroys the enemy because he hates the praise we offer to God.

As we continue reading in 2 Chronicles 20, we find this: "At the very moment they began to sing and give praise, the Lord caused the armies of Ammon, Moab, and Mount Seir to start fighting among themselves. The armies of Moab and Ammon turned against their allies from Mount Seir and killed every one of them. After they had destroyed the army of Seir, they began attacking each other. So, when the army of Judah arrived at the lookout point in the wilderness, all they saw were dead bodies lying on the ground as far as they could see. Not a single one of the enemy had escaped." (2 Chronicles 20:22-24)

Who wants to praise God with me today?

Day 64

Let's Hunt for Buried Treasure

Numbers 4-5 / Mark 12:15-37/ Psalm 48 / Proverbs 10:26

I'm not sure why the Bible is making me laugh this week, but it is! Proverbs 10:26 caught my attention this time.

> "Lazy people irritate their employers,
> like vinegar to the teeth or smoke in the eyes."

Of course, it's not funny when someone is lazy; it personally drives me crazy. The part of imagining vinegar hitting your teeth or smoke hitting your eyes though... well, at least the part of vinegar hitting your teeth; I feel that pain! Have you ever ingested straight vinegar? Then you know what I'm talking about.

What about the lazy part? As you've all read and heard, I'm a Navy brat. My dad served 21 years and retired as a Commander. I was taught to work hard from a young age. I had my first job at 16, and not just any job. I had my own business as a piano teacher. I had 20 students with ages ranging from childhood to adult.

My dad taught me that first year to do my own taxes and report my income. He had me pay my own car insurance on the little 1967 grey Vega I drove (yes, manual 4-speed transmission). We were taught not to let grass grow under our feet. I have never understood anyone who didn't work as hard. It's no surprise I would marry a man with an unmatched work ethic.

To me, laziness doesn't apply only to physical work. We can be spiritually lazy, emotionally lazy, lazy in our thinking or in our desire to be informed. There are many kinds of laziness.

What else does the Bible say about people who are lazy? As it turns out, the Bible has much to say about the lazy versus the diligent. There are so many verses, I don't have room to list them all. I encourage you to look up some verses for yourself.

A great one to start with is the story of the talents in Matthew 25:14-30. For the sake of space, I'll summarize the story.

A man was leaving on a long trip, so he called together his servants and left them in charge of various parts of his estate. He left one with ten talents, one with five talents and one with 1 talent, according to their ability and experience.

When he returned, the two with ten and five talents had worked hard and earned more, while the servant with 1 talent had simply buried it without any investment.

The man was excited at the hard work of the first two, but angry with the laziness of the third.

Do you have talents and gifts that you've invested in, allowing them to grow and bless others? Do you have talents that you've buried? Maybe you buried them out of fear, or concern about what others would think. Maybe it was done because you compared yourself to another and felt small.

Whatever the reason, please dig up those gifts, dust them off and ask God to show you how to increase them! There is still time!

Day 65

The Blessing of the Lord

Numbers 6-7 / Mark 12:38-13:13 / Psalm 49 / Proverbs 10:27-28

"May the Lord bless you and protect you.
May the Lord smile on you and be gracious to you.
May the Lord show you His favor and give you His peace."
—Numbers 6:24-26

Let's dig a little deeper into the meaning of these beautiful verses by using the Amplified Version of the Bible.

"The Lord bless you, and keep you [protect you, sustain you and guard you]; the Lord make His face shine upon you [with favor], and be gracious to you [surrounding you with lovingkindness]; the Lord lift up His countenance (face) upon you [with divine approval], and give you peace [a tranquil heart and life]."

This is a blessing we've heard and read many times. There's even a worship song based on this blessing; a song that I deeply enjoy because of the power of the lyrics. And of course, they are powerful because they are taken straight from scripture.

How many times are we moved to speak blessings over others? And how many times do we actually speak those blessings aloud? We're sometimes quick to speak the negative things that we notice about others, but how often are we able to look beyond what we see and speak heartfelt words of kindness and grace?

I think it would take a great deal of faith to begin to call things that are not as though they were and speak that blessing! (taken from Romans 4:17)

134

Are you willing to do that for someone today? I encourage you to speak the things over them that you see in the Spirit realm, but that may not be showing up in the natural world. I also pray that as you read this blessing, you first take it in and pray it over yourself, then pray the words over someone else.

I bless you today!

Day 66

Giving Thanks Carries Weight

Numbers 8-9 / Mark 13:14-37 / Psalm 50 / Proverbs 10:29-30

There were many directions I could have taken with today's readings. And I thought about talking about our need to be on guard, stay alert, and watch for Him! While that would have been a great topic, I found myself drawn to two phrases in Psalm 50.

The two phrases are mostly the same. Verse 14 states "Make thankfulness your sacrifice to God..." and verse 23 states ". . . giving thanks is a sacrifice that truly honors me."

Has anyone considered that giving thanks is a sacrifice? When I'd rather complain, I may choose to give thanks. When I'd rather be angry or negative, I may choose to give thanks.

When I make this choice, I am truly honoring the Lord. What does it mean to honor the Lord?

When I looked up the word "honor" in the Strong's Concordance it is the word "Kabad", which is defined as "heavy or weighty". It can also be defined as "to bear up under anything or to endure adversity."

As I pondered these meanings, I thought of the scales of justice with two plates upon which to balance weights.

What if I find myself in hard circumstances that are weighing me down? There is weight or heaviness to the trial, causing the scales to tip in a negative direction. Conversely, what if I choose to give thanks to God in my circumstance? Is the other side of the scale now balanced? Or is it heavier? I guess that's up to the "weight" of my thanksgiving.

I have a feeling we can give thanks in such a manner as to cause the scales to tip in our favor! Half-hearted thanksgiving won't work because the scales will still be tipped negatively. If we want to tip the scales in our favor, we must commit to extravagant thanks!

This reminds me of a scripture in 1 Thessalonians 5:18 which states, "Be thankful in all circumstances, for this is God's will for you who belong to Christ Jesus."

What are you facing today? Allow your giving of thanks to tip the scales in your favor!

Day 67

We Are Made Perfect

Numbers 10:1-11:23 / Mark 14:1-21 / Psalm 51 / Proverbs 10:31-32

Psalm 51 is a familiar Psalm. It is the one that was David's prayer after his sin with Bathsheba. Many Jesus followers have used this Psalm as a prayer of contrition and repentance. The imagery is beautiful and filled with hope, especially in the face of our sin.

Verse 1 reads, "Have mercy on me, O God, because of Your unfailing love. Because of Your great compassion, blot out the stain of my sins. Verse 4a reads, "Against You, and You alone, have I sinned."

Let's first acknowledge that we are now made righteous through the blood of Jesus Christ. That means we are already clean, and we may approach God from that place of being right with Him. However, we must still go to Him for forgiveness when we become aware of sin.

When we approach Him, He's not standing angrily before us with a big stick waiting to bring punishment. He stands as a loving Father, smiling and ready to forgive us. He is ready to blot out our sin. What does it mean for Him to do that?

"Blot out" is defined as "erase, abolish, destroy. Also, to blot out from memory."

"I will never again remember their sins."
—Hebrews 8:12

When we belong to Christ, we have been forgiven and we are made perfect through His sacrifice. In addition to wanting to for-

138

give us, He wants us to submit to being conformed to His image. We are made righteous, and we are becoming more like Him. These two truths exist together. When the Father looks at us, He sees the perfection of His Son.

Give Him thanks today, knowing you are made perfect and righteous because of Jesus Christ!

Day 68

How Do We Learn Humility?

Numbers 11:24-13:33 / Mark 14:22-52 / Psalm 52 / Proverbs 11:1-3

I've read the Old Testament stories many times, but this is the first time I saw a connection between Moses' humility and that being the reason God met with him face to face. This is what God says of Moses.

> "Of all my house, he is the one I trust.
> I speak to him face to face, clearly, and not in riddles!
> He sees the LORD as He is."
> —Numbers 12:7-8

I've always been envious that Moses got to see God face to face. He's the only one in scripture, at least in my memory, who could do so. One day in Heaven, I will see Him face to face. But Moses saw God face to face in his earthly body. I'll have to wait for my Heavenly body to see God this way.

There's another scripture I've always loved that speaks to this yearning to see God. It's part of the beatitudes from Matthew 5. Verse 8 reads, "Blessed are the pure in heart, for they shall see God."

I have many favorite verses, but this may be at the top. I can't wait to see God. Yes, I've seen His work all around me. I've heard His voice and felt His touch. But I want to see Him with my own eyes. The thought of this creates an intense longing to know Him as He knows me. Wow, what a day that will be!

140

Let's look back at Moses' humility for a minute. Verse 3 of Numbers 12 says, "Now Moses was very humble – more humble than any other person on earth."

If I want to see and experience God, maybe I should explore this humility thing, so let's see what it means. Let's go look it up!

This is the Bible definition I found "commonly with the added notion of a lowly, pious, and modest mind, which prefers to bear injuries rather than return them."

My husband Jeff is this way, but sometimes I prefer to defend myself or get even. I guess I have a lot to learn about humility.

My next question is, "How do I learn humility?" I'd say that's done through practice. I must first be aware of my fault, then in repentance work through the process of renewing myself to align with God's view.

I'm sure Moses learned humility throughout his life. He was first given up by his mother to save his life, then raised in Pharaoh's household, then made aware of his Hebrew ancestry. Then God had him spend 40 years in the desert as a shepherd. That would be a great place to learn humility.

And God knew Moses would need to be humble to be able to lead the people of Israel into freedom.

Scripture says that Jesus learned obedience (and humility) through the things He suffered. Hebrews 5:8

That's a lot to think about!

Day 69

Battle Before Blessing

Numbers 14:1-15:16 / Mark 14:53-72 / Psalm 53 / Proverbs 11:4

"It is a rich land flowing with milk and honey."
—Numbers 14:8b

What a strange saying! What does it mean? I've heard this read from scripture, and read it myself, since I started reading the KJV Bible at an early age. Yes, I was reading that difficult to understand version as a little girl. Let's take a story break so I can share that with you!

When I started researching home schooling for my own children, I asked my mom whether I had learned by sight words or phonics. She told me that I had not learned either of these ways. She said no one taught me to read; I simply began reading one day straight from the KJV Bible. How can that be?

She said, and I'm sure this is what allowed me to learn, that my Granddaddy Wheeler read to me every day from the time I came home from the hospital until we moved to PA when I was about 7-8 months old. We lived with them while my dad was in the Mediterranean for 6 months with the Navy.

Maybe there's more to the story of my learning to read, but that's all I know. I also somehow have an innate understanding of word meanings based on their Greek and Latin roots, and no one taught me that either. A God-given gift? Maybe!

Let's get back to looking at the meaning of milk and honey. When we read this phrase in scripture, is it literal or figurative? I

142

think it's both and that's proven when looking it up in the Strong's Concordance. Here's what I found.

"Milk" is defined as "milk, sour milk, and cheese. Also – abundance of the land, to make the wealth of nations one's own, claim for oneself."

"Honey" is defined as "honey or honeycomb. Also – honey of grapes or new wine. Also – used of very pleasant discourse." (This definition causes me to think about fellowship with God and one another.)

Not only was God promising physical provision of food, but He was also letting the Israelites know they would inherit the best of the land, the riches, and that they would have a time of peace and rest among each other and with Him. At least that's how I interpret this.

Yes, they were going to have to fight the "giants" in the land first – battle before blessing – and that generation would have to die out because of their unbelief, but their children would inherit the promise!

And the same is true for us. We often must battle some giants to receive our blessing. I say, let's go get some milk and honey!

Day 70

This is What I Believe

Numbers 15:17-16:40 / Mark 15 / Psalm 54 / Proverbs 11:5-6

Who can read the story of Jesus's trial, abuse, and crucifixion without being emotionally moved? It wrecks me every time. Even if I set aside the fact that Jesus was God in the flesh, and the reason He came was to die, the story is a brutal one.

But factor in His perfection, innocence and love for us and it's unimaginable that He did what He did. After considering these things, I want to offer you some foundational doctrine in the form of the Apostles' Creed. This is what I believe...

I believe in God, the Father almighty,
Creator of Heaven and earth.

I believe in Jesus Christ, his only Son, our Lord,
Who was conceived by the Holy Spirit,
And born of the virgin Mary.

He suffered under Pontius Pilate,
Was crucified, died, and was buried.
He descended to hell.

The third day he rose again from the dead.
He ascended to Heaven.
And is seated at the right hand of God the Father almighty.
From there he will come to judge the living and the dead.

I believe in the Holy Spirit,
The holy church,
The communion of saints,
The forgiveness of sins,
The resurrection of the body,
And the life everlasting. Amen.

Reading this also moves my heart and faith in a major way.

Day 71

What do Wish for Your Enemies?

Numbers 16:41-18:32 / Mark 16 / Psalm 55 / Proverbs 11:7

How are we supposed to deal with people who irritate and make us angry? How do we deal with people who appear to be enemies?

I think it's important to define the word "enemies" before we continue. The word for "enemy" is *oyeb* in Hebrew and is defined as "an adversary, someone who persecutes or hates you."

We may or may not have true enemies, but as Jesus followers we share one common enemy and that is the devil.

In our reading, it is interesting to see the vast difference in how Moses and Aaron routinely handled the situation when the people of Israel were behaving as enemies toward their leadership and toward God, and how David addresses the topic of enemies in his prayers in the Psalms.

In reading the Old Testament, I remember at least three times so far this year that Moses has fallen face down on the ground when the people are being rebellious, and the Lord is threatening to kill them. Moses responds by asking God for mercy when the people have sinned, even when they were revolting against his leadership. We could learn a lot from this example.

David, on the other hand, wrote this when his enemies were harassing him in Psalm 55:15: "Let death stalk my enemies; let the grave swallow them alive, for evil makes its home within them."

There appears to be no mercy in David's declaration!

When I'm reading the Old Testament writings, I must remember that these events happened pre-Cross. They occurred before Jesus came and brought grace and forgiveness through His sacrifice.

146

Moses acted as an intermediary, something that in God's justice is required. Moses' actions kept God from wiping His people out. But this intermediation had to be done again and again because it lacked perfection.

When Jesus suffered, died, and rose again, His was a perfect sacrifice with no need to be regularly repeated.

I want to go back to Moses's response. What if we, when persecuted or spoken evil of or to, chose to fall face down on the ground? I see this as putting aside our pain and anger and choosing to pray, asking God to work in the situation.

I'll be the first to admit that I am passionate and quick tempered, and I have much to learn in this area. What about you? How do you respond when attacked or accused?

Lord, help us show mercy.

Day 72

A Collection of Tears

Numbers 19-20 / Luke 1:1-25 / Psalm 56 / Proverbs 11:8

"You keep track of all my sorrows.
You have collected all my tears in your bottle.
You have recorded each one in your book."
—Psalm 56:8

It was on this day in the year 2021 that we said our final good-byes to our beloved son-in-law Bradley. Our family attended Catholic Mass with Bradley's family and friends in Louisiana, and it was very honoring both of Bradley and of his faith in Christ. Then we went together to his family's mausoleum and interred his ashes.

It was hard losing Bradley, but it was even harder watching my daughter suffer. Loss is overwhelming. Grief changes us.

We never forget the loss, and while the grief gets softer over time, it doesn't totally disappear.

Life begins and life ends but we may still bless the Name of the Lord. We are so thankful to each one who prayed, who sent thoughts, etc. during that difficult season. We're grateful for you, and we're grateful God collects our tears.

Bradley, until we meet again; I know you are enjoying your Heavenly home.

And to those who have lost someone, I understand and I'm sorry for your pain. I hope my prayers reach you today and give you some comfort and hope.

Day 73

The Life-altering "Yes"

Numbers 21:1-22:20 / Luke 1:26-56 / Psalm 57 /Proverbs 11:9-11

In Luke 1:38 Mary responded, "I am the Lord's servant. May everything you have said about me come true."

How many of us would be willing to respond this way if God sent an angel to tell us our life was going to be greatly altered?

God didn't ask Mary whether or not she wanted this life intervention; He simply saw her willing heart, chose her and sent His messenger.

Mary's "yes" to God was going to bring shame on her and her family, but she still consented. She knew the risks; she knew the consequences. Yet she chose to be God's vessel.

Would you have done the same? I must wonder, would I?

God has asked many things of me in my life, as I'm sure He has you. Sometimes I've said "yes" and sometimes I've ignored what I heard because I didn't think I could do what He was asking. Have I ever said a flat "no"? I don't remember, but I probably have.

And that's sad because if God is asking, it's part of His perfect plan. The course of travel will be both difficult and fun, and the outcome will probably be unexpected, but we can be assured we are walking the path He designed for us. I believe there's no safer place to walk.

What is God asking of you today? Will you say "yes?" I promise it's the best "yes" you'll ever utter!

149

Day 74

What We Speak Matters

Numbers 22:21-23:30 / Luke 1:57-80 / Psalm 58 / Proverbs 11:12-13

I appreciate prophecy. I crave hearing God's voice, whether in my own ear or through someone else. That's why I am fascinated by the story of Zechariah, Elizabeth, and their newborn son John.

Remember, it's been nine months since Zechariah came out of the temple unable to speak. Everyone knew he had encountered God, but no one knew why.

Then Elizabeth became pregnant, going into seclusion for five months. I've wondered why she secluded herself. Was it because she was old and not ready to announce her pregnancy? At some point everyone was going to know, and some would connect her pregnancy with Zechariah's temple encounter.

Elizabeth's baby recognized his cousin Jesus while they were both still in the womb. Remember John leapt inside his mother when Mary greeted them. Who says babies can't vastly impact things prophetically!

Now, the 9-month period has passed, the baby has been born and it's time to circumcise and name him in a traditional ceremony. When asked his name, Elizabeth answers "John", which shocks everyone because there is no family member named John. But Zechariah calls for writing implements and confirms the name.

And his voice returns. 9 months and 8 days (give or take) of silence has been broken. What's the first thing out of Zechariah's mouth? A prophetic utterance about the deliverance from evil for

150

God's people. Then he turns to his 8-day old son and speaks his destiny over him, bringing me near tears...

How often have I spoken my children's and grandchildren's destiny over them? Am I even aware of their destinies? To a great degree, the answer is yes, I am aware, though I only see in part.

Bottom line... our spoken words carry great weight.

What are you speaking about yourself and others? I challenge you to listen to what you say this week. Are you speaking life, health, peace, and destiny? If not, it's never too late to begin.

Day 75

Blessed be the Name of the Lord

Numbers 24-25 / Luke 2:1-35 / Psalm 59 / Proverbs 11:14

We've talked before about how our worship is warfare – about how when we choose to worship and praise our awesome and mighty God, the enemy hates it and runs.

There was a time in the story of healing from a car accident and surgery when I was so overwhelmed with the pain and depression that I couldn't pray or worship. What did I do? I turned up the music!

In March 2014, I had surgery for a ruptured disc from our car accident in December 2013 and my life shifted dramatically during this season. As I was confined to home recovering, I became hopeless. It was a very difficult season, but I knew that worship would help.

One day I sensed a dark cloud gathered over me (enemy oppression is real) and it was as if the devil was yelling at me because the sound in the spirit was so loud and intrusive.

I had created 2 worship playlists with about 40 songs each that I played continuously. When the enemy thought he would yell at me, when his voice got louder, the music had to be cranked up! And it worked! Did you know little "d" (the devil) hates worship? LOL! I made him run that day and I'm not sorry.

So, when I read in Luke about the armies of Heaven praising God and saying, "Glory to God in the highest Heaven, and peace on earth to those with whom God is pleased" (Luke 2:13-14), I was excited to learn that even Heaven's army praises God. I always thought of the army as a battle only type of entity. But it would make sense that they would do warfare in worship as we are called to do the same.

152

If Heaven's armies, with Jesus as their captain, can worship in warfare, I must do the same and I must do so often. "I will bless the Lord at all times – His praise will continually be in my mouth." Psalm 34:1

At. All. Times.

When I'm happy, sad, angry, confused, in tears, in pain, in sorrow, in joy, in darkness, in light, and in every circumstance.

In Job 1:20-21 Job stood up and tore his robe in grief. Then he shaved his head and fell to the ground to worship.

He said, "I came naked from my mother's womb, and I will be naked when I leave. The Lord gave me what I had, and the Lord has taken it away. Praise the name of the Lord!"

I need to work on my response being to praise the name of the Lord, no matter what happens. I'm not saying we don't cry, grieve or suffer, but at some point, we must come to the realization that God is good even when we don't understand.

Do I understand why my daddy left earlier than I expected? No.

Do I understand why our son-in-law Bradley left us way too young? No.

But I know God is good and He is worthy to be praised. If you're not "there" yet, I understand and there is much grace. However, when you've processed, consider turning your heart to worship and see if a burden is not lifted from your soul. It's helped me, and I believe it will also help you.

Blessed by Your Name, Lord

Day 76

He Who Knew No Sin

Numbers 26:1-51 / Luke 2:36-52 / Psalm 60 / Proverbs 11:15

Never mind that I'm a woman, I think it would be fun to name a clan after myself as they did in Numbers. If I go based on my reading, since my name is Maria, my clan's name would be Mariaite. What is your clan's name?

The only difference I noticed where the nations didn't simply add "ite" was if the name ended in "ah". In this case, the "ah" is dropped and "ite" is added. After a little fun, let's explore today's revelation from the reading!

Of Jesus as a child, it is said in Luke 2:40, "There the child grew up healthy and strong. He was filled with wisdom, and God's favor was on Him." Then later in Luke 2:52, when Jesus was twelve it is said, "Jesus grew in wisdom and stature and in favor with God and all the people."

For those of you with children, can you imagine having raised a child who did not sin? Scripture clearly teaches in 2 Corinthians 5:21 that Jesus knew no sin. What would it have been like to teach a child who was filled with God's wisdom and had God's favor?

Favor is defined as "grace, of the merciful kindness by which God, exerting his holy influence upon souls, turns them to Christ, keeps, strengthens, increases them in Christian faith, knowledge, affection, and kindles them to the exercise of the Christian virtues."

Imagine if you talked and they listened. You taught them things and they quickly learn. You gave them instructions and they obeyed. Compare that to Mary and Joseph's other children. They had to have

154

noticed a massive difference when raising the One who knew no sin, and the others who were born with a sin nature.

I can imagine that even though Mary had been visited by the angel who told her who Jesus was, that she didn't fully understand what that meant. After all, she was a mother who had a baby boy that she loved very much. This had never happened before (a virgin conception and birth) and would never happen again. I bet Mary's mind was reeling, trying to understand what this meant. Mine would have been!

But remember what is soon to come. Jesus will grow into a man who will never marry. He will have a short life of only 33 years, then he will be murdered. Mary's perfect baby boy will be killed though He is innocent. I wonder how Mary reconciled that injustice in her heart?

She would have to forgive, and I'm sure she remembered her son's teachings on forgiveness. But how hard that would have been.

When you read scripture, do you ever put yourself in the place of those about whom you read? Do you remind yourself that they were just like us? Sometimes we separate those in scripture as better than ourselves, but they were not. They simply lived in a different time. Yet we are still able to learn from their example.

So, though you may wish at times that your children were perfect like Jesus was, don't forget the things He and His mother suffered, and He did that for our sake. He gave His life willingly.

Hug and kiss your beautiful, yet imperfect children, and thank Jesus today for His gift of eternal life.

Day 77

A Gracious Woman

Numbers 26:52-28:15 / Luke 3:1-22 / Psalm 61 / Proverbs 11:16-17

Women in the Bible are fascinating and there are too many stories to recount here. Women in the east have for centuries been seen more as property than people of equal value with men. But God does not see male or female; He sees us as equal in His Kingdom.

That's why I love the decision that God led Moses to make on behalf of five sisters in Numbers. Their names were Mahlah, Noah, Hoglah, Milcah, and Tirzah. When it was time to draw lots and divide the land among the clans as the Israelites prepared to enter the Promised Land, the girls spoke up on behalf of their father's household, not wanting his name to disappear from his clan.

I admire their boldness in asking. I admire Moses' willingness to bring the case before the Lord. I am also grateful the Lord decided in their favor and granted they would have the land their father would have inherited. It proves God's heart toward women.

Psalm 61:16a reads, "A gracious woman gains respect."

Gracious is defined as "full of grace, elegance, favor, and charm."

Think of a woman who knows how to behave and speak appropriate to the situation because she has had a long season of learning such things.

The phrase "gains respect" is defined as "to lay hold of or retain honor, dignity, and reputation." This definition has an active connotation.

These two together make me think of a woman who knows her value, and her worth and she knows how to boldly step forward to

156

garner what is rightfully hers. She knows what belongs to her because she has heard God speak it to her. She is not afraid to take hold of what God has promised, again because she has heard God speak to her and she trusts Him.

Do you have promises, inheritances, hopes and dreams that are lying dormant waiting for you to "take them up"? If so, may I encourage you today to prayerfully take steps toward what God has already given you? Remember, if He has promised, it is yours. It's not that it "will be" yours. It is yours.

Be a bold woman of God, and lay hold of that which Christ laid hold of for you! After all, it is to bring Him glory.

Day 78

One Perfect Offering

Numbers 28:16-29:40 / Luke 3:23-38 / Psalm 62 / Proverbs 11:18-19

The Bible tells us that Christ died once for all men, and when Jesus came, He fulfilled every letter of the law.

If you've ever read the Old Testament books that give details about all the sacrifices required under the law you would become thankful for two things. One, that you did not live in a time when you had to abide by these daily, monthly, and special holy day sacrifices. Two, that Jesus Christ was the perfect sacrifice, taking away all the sins of the world.

The more I read, the more I wonder how the people of Israel had time to do anything other than prepare animals, flour, olive oil and wine for the unceasing sacrifices. Think about it, they had to harvest the wheat, beat off the chaff, store the grain, and when it was time grind it by hand without electricity and fancy appliances.

They had to choose the perfect animals with no blemishes, then kill and butcher them according to the prescribed laws. They had to harvest the olives, and press the oil, again by hand. They had to harvest the grapes, press the grapes, and ferment them into homemade wine. Are you tired yet? I am!

Multiply this by millions of people and thousands of households and this process was literally never-ending. Imagine the amount of cattle required. Imagine the smell of cattle all around you, all day every day. The fire on the altar, the smoke, the smell of burning meat. I'm sorry to belabor this, but the enormity of what was required must be felt so the cost of what Jesus brought can be more fully appreciated.

158

The people of God were looking to the day when Messiah would come and rescue His people. Never mind that some of them thought He would free them from Roman rule and set up an earthly kingdom (we do tend to think in human terms first).

When Messiah came, not everyone recognized Him for who He was; even those who had studied the prophetic passages in scripture all their lives. The One Who was perfect came to rescue the imperfect. He Who knew no sin became sin for us so that we might be made right with God.

Hebrews 10:1-10 is too good not to include here...

"The old system under the law of Moses was only a shadow, a dim preview of the good things to come, not the good things themselves. The sacrifices under that system were repeated again and again, year after year, but they were never able to provide perfect cleansing for those who came to worship.

If they could have provided perfect cleansing, the sacrifices would have stopped, for the worshipers would have been purified once for all time, and their feelings of guilt would have disappeared.

But instead, those sacrifices actually reminded them of their sins year after year.

For it is not possible for the blood of bulls and goats to take away sins.

That is why, when Christ came into the world, he said to God,

'You did not want animal sacrifices or sin offerings. But you have given me a body to offer.

You were not pleased with burnt offerings or other offerings for sin.'

Then I said, 'Look, I have come to do your will, O God—as is written about me in the Scriptures.'

First, Christ said, 'You did not want animal sacrifices or sin offerings or burnt offerings or other offerings for sin, nor were you pleased with them' (though they are required by the law of Moses).

Then he said, 'Look, I have come to do your will.' He cancels the first covenant in order to put the second into effect.

For God's will was for us to be made holy by the sacrifice of the body of Jesus Christ, once for all time."

Jesus, I'm thankful for Your sacrifice.

Day 79

Lead Me Along Straight Paths

Numbers 30-31 / Luke 4:1-30 / Psalm 63 / Proverbs 11:20-21

Truth and integrity are becoming rare in the world today, and distinguishing truth from lies is becoming harder to discern. Proverbs 11:20 states, "The LORD detests people with crooked hearts, but he delights in those with integrity."

The term "crooked heart" is interesting, but what does it mean? Before we look it up, when I think of a crooked path, I think of one that takes many twists and turns. Or when I think of someone who doesn't want to speak truth (or doesn't know truth), I think of someone who dodges questions or who doesn't speak clearly.

Truth, on the other hand, appears as more of a straight path, although it may perhaps take some gentle curves along the way. These pictures are simply my own interpretation of what a truthful, verses a lying, path might look like if drawn. That's what we artists do, we visualize as we read.

What does it look like to compare a crooked heart with someone who has integrity? That may seem straight forward, but let's dig into the subtleties as I love to do!

A "crooked heart" is defined as "twisted, distorted, crooked, perverse, perverted, deceitful and false in mind, will, understanding and thinking."

Integrity is defined as "sound, wholesome, unimpaired, innocent, having integrity. Also, what is complete or entirely in accord with truth and fact."

Right away you're probably wondering, as am I, if anyone would fall fully into either category. We know some people who appear to be evil and some who appear to be good and honest. But the truth is, apart from Christ in us, none of us is good. Yes, there are people who try to do good and people who don't care and enjoy evil (I know that's hard to imagine, but it's true).

If you're trying to live right, that's a good thing. But right living alone will not gain eternal life and reconciliation with God. We must go through Jesus Christ to be made right with God. There is no other path.

If you're concerned with integrity, you either belong to Christ or you may be on a path to finding Him as He is the only One who is good.

Today, I bless you with integrity and no matter where your heart may lie regarding Christ, I pray your path leads you daily to Him.

Day 80

A Boat Full of Blessings

Numbers 32:1-33:39 / Luke 4:31-5:11 / Psalm 64 / Proverbs 11:22

When Jesus borrowed Simon's boat, asking him to push it out into the water, did He already have in mind to do the miracle of loading the boats with fish? Was Jesus aware that His Father was choosing these men to be His disciples and walk with Him the next 3 years?

I believe that in God's Kingdom there are no accidents, no coincidences. God is a careful planner who does all He does with great intention and purpose. I believe Jesus knew these men would follow Him. And I believe He was excitedly looking forward to overfilling their boats after He completed speaking to the crowd. I bet He was smiling on the inside the whole time! I would have been.

Do you believe God has good things in store for you? Things that He planned even before you were born. Is He an angry, stingy God or a God who can't wait to load you with blessings? Let's answer according to scripture.

Ephesians 2:8-10 reads, "God saved you by his grace when you believed. And you can't take credit for this; it is a gift from God. Salvation is not a reward for the good things we have done, so none of us can boast about it. For we are God's masterpiece. He has created us anew in Christ Jesus, so we can do the good things he planned for us long ago."

Psalm 68:19 reads, "Blessed be the Lord, who daily loads us with benefits, the God of our salvation! Selah."

2 Peter 1:3-4 reads, "By his divine power, God has given us everything we need for living a godly life. We have received all of this

164

by coming to know him, the one who called us to himself by means of his marvelous glory and excellence. And because of his glory and excellence, he has given us great and precious promises. These are the promises that enable you to share his divine nature and escape the world's corruption caused by human desires."

Based on the above verses, I think my assessment of Jesus's thoughts and intentions is correct. He delights in giving us all we need! I think He was excited to bless Simon and the others with a great number of fish! And He wants to bless you in the same way. Maybe not with a boat full of fish, but with something that is specific to you.

Watch and wait for it!

Day 81

Two Important Daily Tasks

Numbers 33:40-35:34 / Luke 5:12-28 / Psalm 65 / Proverbs 11:23

Jesus's wisdom fascinates me as we read through the Gospels. He was so dependent upon His Father and Holy Spirit, that they worked together in perfect unison as difficult situations arose. They worked together as the truth was preached, people were healed and delivered from demons, and as their sins were forgiven.

Prior to Jesus's coming, the forgiveness of sin was done by temple sacrifices, so most who were listening to Jesus were not aware that their long-awaited for Messiah had arrived and was preparing Himself to be the ultimate sacrifice for their sins and their healing.

This is probably why the religious leaders were miffed, angry, whatever you want to call it, when Jesus told the paralyzed man his sins were forgiven. No one had said or done that before!

Of course, the religious leaders didn't express this aloud; they were keeping their evil thoughts within their own hearts. But Jesus knew what they were thinking because Holy Spirit could read their thoughts.

Did you know that Holy Spirit can read the thoughts of men? That's why scripture places such importance on us guarding our hearts and minds, because our actions stem from these two places.

We have the same opportunity for discernment in every situation. We may not be able to read the thoughts of others, but the Holy Spirit can give us insight, both so we're able to combat evil and so we're able to bring encouragement when others have doubts.

166

Have you ever had just the right words at just the right time for someone? Have you wondered how you knew what to say? It's by the discernment and leadership of Holy Spirit that we know things we would not otherwise know.

That's why it's important to be filled with Him daily. Ephesians 6 tells us to put on the full armor of God so we can stand against the enemy. This must also be done daily. Ephesians 5:18 states, "Don't be drunk with wine, because that will ruin your life. Instead, be filled with the Holy Spirit."

These are two of your most important daily tasks, to be filled and put on your armor. This will allow you to walk closely with Holy Spirit so He can direct you each day. How exciting it is to walk in His path each day!

Day 82

Seeds for the Hungry Heart

Numbers 36 – Deuteronomy 1 / Luke 5:29-5:11
Psalm 66 / Proverbs 11:24-26

"Give freely – be generous – refresh others –
and fellowship with sinners."
—Proverbs 11:24-25

I love the stories about the people Jesus chose to spend His free time with, and those He ate and laughed with because He did the unexpected according to social norms of the day. He ate with those who were considered lowly in Jewish society. He ate with tax collectors, prostitutes and sinners.

I believe Jesus's heart was to go where He was needed but also where He and His message would be received and that was not usually to the religious leaders of the day (though there were a few like Nicodemus).

I imagine Jesus to have been both gentle and strong, kind, and full of wisdom and truth. I know He was without sin, so there was no compromise as He spent time with these "outcasts". Remember, He was able to see what was in their hearts, so I think He knew they were ready to hear His message of healing and deliverance. I think He was drawn to those with hungry hearts.

What about you? Who do you spend time with? Are you afraid to be seen with "sinners"? Are you afraid your reputation will be ruined? What if we were more concerned with obeying God and not with what others thought about us? These are some great questions to ask ourselves!

I enjoy all types of people and I love hearing their stories. Every story has pain and triumph, and every person is searching for truth and love.

As a follower of Jesus, I'm able to offer both truth and love, so why would I not choose to spend time with those who need what I have? This allows me to spend time with those who have hungry hearts, whether they know Jesus or not, and it brings me great joy to do so because one never knows when Holy Spirit will allow a seed to be planted or watered. I love to plant seeds and to water those already planted.

1 Corinthians 3:5-9 reads, "After all, who is Apollos? Who is Paul? We are only God's servants through whom you believed the Good News. Each of us did the work the Lord gave us. I planted the seed in your hearts, and Apollos watered it, but it was God who made it grow. It's not important who does the planting, or who does the watering. What's important is that God makes the seed grow. The one who plants and the one who waters work together with the same purpose. And both will be rewarded for their own hard work. For we are both God's workers. And you are God's field. You are God's building."

Let's get out there to plant and water and watch God work. Talk about the great adventure!

Day 83

God is Kind, even to the Wicked

Deuteronomy 2-3 / Luke 6:12-38 / Psalm 67 / Proverbs 11:27

"...for He is kind to those who are unthankful and wicked..."
"Do not judge others, and you will not be judged. Do not
condemn others, or it will all come back against you. Forgive others,
and you will be forgiven. Give, and you will receive."
—Luke 6:35-37

These verses from Luke are sobering. Some of the truth in these verses seems difficult to walk out, and some of the truth contained here has been misinterpreted.

We prefer to "pay back" those who hurt us, but the Lord is kind to the unthankful and wicked. Even if someone does not recognize His kindness, He isn't moved by that. How often are we upset when we do something for someone, and they don't thank us or even notice what we've done? Perhaps we should work on being kind anyway.

What about someone who is truly evil? How hard it is to be kind to an evil person (though most people I've met are not this way). But God sends rain on both the righteous and the unrighteous. Both receive the goodness of the earth and everything God placed here. We don't have to be right with God to enjoy His creation.

This has me considering our judgments. How often do we give or withhold love based on our opinion regarding the worthiness of another? It is not our responsibility to make that decision, but rather we are to do good to all men, especially to those who are part of our household of faith in God.

170

Let's clear up some confusion around the word "judge" because I've heard some interpret this scripture incorrectly.

The word judge is defined as "to pronounce an opinion concerning right and wrong. To be judged, i.e. summoned to trial, that one's case may be examined, and judgment passed upon it. To pronounce judgment, to subject to censure. Of those who act the part of judges or arbiters in matters of common life or pass judgment on the deeds and words of others."

This type of judgment is reserved for God because it is a final judgment that includes sentencing. Think of a court case. Someone comes before the court to be given a sentence concerning their guilt or innocence. The judge is the one who has the final decision on their guilt or innocence. God is the Judge, and He will base a person's guilt or innocence on whether they have received His Son Jesus Christ. Therefore, this is not our role.

We may, however, look at another person's life to determine whether the fruit of their lives appears to be good and from God, or evil and from satan. This process is one of discernment and assists us in knowing who is and is not safe for us to build with in relationship. We must also discern in what spirit others are operating. That will also help us determine whether the relationship will be safe and beneficial.

But again, we are not permitted to be part of a final judgment or sentencing upon another. That is reserved for God's Throne of Judgment.

Our responsibility is to be kind, don't judge, don't condemn, forgive, and give. I know this is sometimes easier said than done, but I encourage you today to find someone to be kind to. Then you can rest in knowing you are behaving like God would have you behave.

Day 84

The Wise Builder

Deuteronomy 4 / Luke 6:39-7:10 / Psalm 68:1-18 / Proverbs 11:28

"Obey {God's decrees and regulations} completely,
and you will display your wisdom and intelligence
among the surrounding nations."
—Deuteronomy 4:6a

"So why do you keep calling me 'Lord, Lord!' when you don't do what I say? I will show you what it's like when someone comes to me, listens to my teaching, and then follows it. It is like a person building a house who digs deep and lays the foundation on solid rock. When the floodwaters rise and break against that house, it stands firm because it is well built. But anyone who hears and doesn't obey is like a person who builds a house right on the ground, without a foundation. When the floods sweep down against that house, it will collapse into a heap of ruins." Luke 6:46-49

Both passages speak about wisdom that is directly tied to obedience to God's Word, which is the same as hearing His voice. This also reminds me of what James 1 states.

"But don't just listen to God's word. You must do what it says. Otherwise, you are only fooling yourselves. For if you listen to the word and don't obey, it is like glancing at your face in a mirror. You see yourself, walk away, and forget what you look like. But if you look carefully into the perfect law that sets you free, and if you do what it says and don't forget what you heard, then God will bless you for doing it." James 1:22-25

Before we can obey, we must hear God speaking. After we hear Him speak, we have a choice to make. We can obey His voice or disregard the truth. When we need wisdom, we can ask God, but what if we don't like His response. Perhaps we think we're not capable of following through with what He's asking. Of course, that's not true: it is Holy Spirit's job to enable us to act upon what we've heard. It is our job to say, "Yes".

Let's look at Luke 6 again. How often have you begun an endeavor and you were not quite sure how to proceed? Maybe you barreled through anyway, and perhaps that was a disaster. What if you asked God for wisdom before you acted?

Do you know that He cares about everything you undertake? All of it. There is nothing too large or too small that He will not listen and offer His direction.

Where and how will you hear that direction? It may be as you read your Bible, or as you pray that you will hear His voice. He may send someone with either the wisdom you need or a direct word from Him to confirm what you've asked for.

Whatever it is you need, whatever your question, whatever difficulty is ahead, remember to ask God for wisdom!

James 1:5-8 reads, "If you need wisdom, ask our generous God, and he will give it to you. He will not rebuke you for asking. But when you ask him, be sure that your faith is in God alone. Do not waver, for a person with divided loyalty is as unsettled as a wave of the sea that is blown and tossed by the wind. Such people should not expect to receive anything from the Lord. Their loyalty is divided between God and the world, and they are unstable in everything they do."

Day 85

We Never Die

Deuteronomy 5-6 / Luke 7:11-35 / Psalm 68:19-35 / Proverbs 11:29-31

Today's encouragement is simple, yet life changing! True life begins only when we accept the gift God gave through His Son Jesus Christ by saying "yes" to His sacrifice on the cross.

Today I want to share some of my favorite verses that support the verse from Psalm 68:20.

"Our God is a God who saves!
The Sovereign Lord rescues us from death."

Death is partially defined as separation from God. For those who belong to Christ, we never experience true death.

2 Corinthians 5:15 states, "He died for everyone so that those who receive his new life will no longer live for themselves. Instead, they will live for Christ, who died and was raised for them."

John 10:28-30 states, "I give them eternal life, and they will never perish. No one can snatch them away from me, for my Father has given them to me, and he is more powerful than anyone else. No one can snatch them from the Father's hand. The Father and I are one."

I know I've shared this before, but I want to share again because it impacted me so deeply. When my dad left earth in Oct 2016, Holy Spirit visited me in a strong way. My first response was to laugh because I knew my daddy was with his Savior. My second response was an abundance of tears because I was going to miss him so much.

174

Holy Spirit also brought a beautiful revelation to my heart that day. He clearly said to me that my daddy did not die but that he had moved from life on earth, to life in Heaven. That helped me so much! I still grieve, but not without hope. I'm thankful for the heritage God has given my family and me – that of faith in Jesus Christ.

I pray you have received this same hope.

Day 86

The Wise One Learns

Deuteronomy 7-8 / Luke 7:37-8:3 / Psalm 69:1-18 / Proverbs 12:1

"To learn, you must love discipline;
it is stupid to hate correction."
—Proverbs 12:1

The word discipline as used in this verse is not referring to structured time with lists and neat piles on your desk. Some of us think that to learn we must be orderly and committed to a regular routine, and while that is true, we must also be teachable and humble, and willing to be corrected.

When the word "discipline" is used in this verse, it is speaking of being willing to be corrected. We must love correction. That means we must be willing to admit we are wrong so we can begin to think differently.

As I continue daily to read through scripture, the Lord is reshaping my doctrine. Over the years I've picked up some beliefs and ways of thinking that didn't quite line up with God's Word. We don't always realize that our thinking doesn't line up with His truth.

Every man and woman only partially understands God's truth. We do the best we can to understand the Bible with the help of Holy Spirit. That's why it's important not only to spend time with other Jesus followers studying what God said, but we must also read the Bible for ourselves.

If you've never read the Bible for yourself, I'd love to encourage you to do so. If you have questions, find another believer who knows the Bible and ask for help. Yes, reading the Bible is a form of discipline, and a very important one for Jesus followers.

The Bible just told us we are "stupid" if we hate correction. The word "stupid" is one of those words we were not allowed to say as pastor's kids; neither were our kids allowed to say it. As a result of those limitations in childhood, when I read the word in the above verse, I laughed out loud!

What does the word stupid mean? In this context it means "foolish" which is the opposite of wise. When we read our Bibles, we will find those areas where we have believed a lie. In that moment we must allow our thinking to be corrected. Only the humble will allow correction and a reshaping of thinking.

I suppose we should reconcile ourselves to being humble and teachable. Because I sure don't want to be stupid and foolish!

Day 87

Who is Good?

Deuteronomy 9-10 / Luke 8:4-21 / Psalm 69:19-36 / Proverbs 12:2-3

"You must recognize that the LORD your God is not
giving you this good land because you are good,
for you are not – you are a stubborn people."
—Deuteronomy 9:6

"The Lord approves of those who are good..." Proverbs 12:2a

When I saw the word "good" repeated in my reading today, I had to investigate. When I see or hear the word "good", I'm immediately reminded of this verse found in Mark 10:18 and again in Luke 18:19.

"Why do you call me good?" Jesus answered.
"No one is good – except God alone."

There is a lot to explore in the different uses of this one word. Let's compare the different definitions.

"Good land" is defined as "good, pleasant, agreeable".

"Good" people (versus stubborn ones) refers to "justice, righteousness and prosperity of people".

"Good" in Proverbs is the same word as found in Deuteronomy so has the same meaning of "good, pleasant, agreeable".

"Good" in Mark and Luke is defined as "of good nature, pleasant, agreeable, joyful, happy, excellent, upright, honorable".

Looking at all of this reminds me that the verses in Mark and

178

Luke are foundationally true in that only God is good. Scripture tells us plainly that we are born with a sin nature, our old Adam nature, and that apart from being renewed through a relationship with Christ, we cannot be made right with God.

Apart from the sacrifice Jesus made, we could not have a relationship with God who is Good.

Yes, I've met "good" people who did not know Jesus Christ. They are kind, moral people that would give you the shirt off their own back. And I'm thankful for kind people. I'd much rather interact with a kind than a mean person – who wouldn't? But at the end of the day, it is not our kindness or goodness that gains us anything from an eternal perspective.

I strive to be kind and good to all, but without the influence of Jesus in my heart, I could not attain a goodness that would assure me of going to Heaven when I die. Because of that, I'm thankful for what Jesus did on the cross.

Jesus, I thank you for your sacrifice on the cross so that I could be made right with God, and so that I can show the kindness and love You have given me to those around me.

If someone says to me that I'm a kind or good person, I will point them to Jesus who lives in me. He is the One who is kind and good.

Day 88

The Excellent (Warrior) Wife

Deuteronomy 11-12 / Luke 8:22-39 / Psalm 70 / Proverbs 12:4

"An excellent wife is the crown of her husband, but she
who shames him is like rottenness in his bones."
—Proverbs 12:4

Those of you who are married, did you know the weight you carry in the home and in your marriage? Do you know the responsibility before God? There is much said in Proverbs about the excellent wife and woman, and it may seem a heavy load to carry, but with time, obedience and patience we are all capable of becoming more excellent.

I love the meaning of the word "excellent". Excellent (the Hebrew word "chayil") is defined as "strength, power, might (especially warlike), valor. To show oneself strong, to display valor. Leader of the army, soldiers. Ability, hence, wealth, riches – to acquire wealth. Virtue, uprightness, integrity, also fitness. The strength of a tree, spoken poetically of its fruits."

In the Passion Translation, we find this explanation for the term "virtuous wife": "There is an amazing Hebrew word used here. It is more commonly used to describe warriors, champions, and mighty ones. Many translations read 'an excellent wife.' But the meaning of the Hebrew word 'chayil' is better translated 'an army that is wealthy', 'strong', 'mighty', 'powerful', 'with substance', 'valiant', 'virtuous', or 'worthy.'"

I identify with this excellent and virtuous warrior woman!

I want to share the story about something my dad saw of me in the Spirit one day during worship. It is one of my favorite times of being identified by an important man in my life (and we must not allow just anyone to identify us!). He came to me after our service in which I had led worship and told me this, "I saw you in the Spirit during worship today, and you were standing with your sword held high." Yes, I was. And yes, I do. I aspire to always be ready.

I've spoken of the warrior before, and it is something I identify with easily because my dad was a warrior, and he passed this spirit on to me. My three adult children have this same excellent, warrior characteristic.

Some warriors are brave and bold, and some are quiet and steady. I don't think your personality type is what makes you a warrior. I think you are a warrior if you have submitted yourself to the will and way of Jesus Christ.

The warrior woman makes no apologies for the place she stands in Christ. She guards the truth, as well as those who are weak. She speaks with both truth and justice.

What kind of man must it require to allow his wife to be excellent? A humble and strong one! Only a man who is secure and fully submitted to God himself will nurture and encourage such strength in his wife, and my husband Jeff is such a man.

He encourages and champions me in all that God has placed within me. He is not intimidated by or afraid of who I am. And there are times I seem a little odd to some people. Jeff accepts me as I am, and I am grateful.

If you're not sure whether you are yet excellent, may I assure you that if you are in Christ, you're well on your way. It's a matter of saying "yes" to His plan and purpose for you. So, say "yes" and let the adventure begin!

Day 89

A God Encounter

Deuteronomy 13-15 / Luke 8:40-9:6 / Psalm 71 /Proverbs 12:5-7

> "But Jesus said, 'Someone deliberately touched me,
> for I felt healing power go out from me.'"
> —Luke 8:46

> "Let me proclaim Your power to this new generation,
> Your mighty miracles to all who come after me."
> —Psalm 71:18b

I was born in 1962, saved in 1968 at age five, baptized in water at age 7 and baptized in the Holy Spirit for the first time at age 11. I've shared some of my experiences with the presence of God. I've experienced and witnessed both God's presence and His power.

In the 1970's we experienced the Jesus Movement, where the "hippies" were being saved, delivered from drugs, receiving salvation, and being filled with God's Spirit. I was witness to what was a chaotically beautiful time in history. As I've aged, I've watched as the church has become more sedate, and I've longed for my children to experience the same supernatural power I have.

I've not just longed for this; I've prayed and believed God for it. And I believe we are seeing the edges of a reformation in the Church right now. I won't share the story of another, but someone very close to me is experiencing some incredible words from God's Spirit, breakthroughs and provision. This is something I've waited to see and it's happening! The power of God is moving.

182

I don't seek God's power just for the sake of power; I seek it because people's lives are eternally changed in the wake of His coming. I can't imagine Heaven without those who are most important to me, especially my family. And since there's nothing I can do to change anyone, I must pray and wait for God to grab their attention: that's exactly what He's doing! There is no excitement that compares with witnessing a life changed by the supernatural power of God!

Have you ever prayed for someone and been aware that the power of God was present to influence their situation? I don't know what Jesus felt as the woman touched Him and received healing for her bleeding, but I know God's power is not just a concept. It is a tangible flow of divine energy.

I've shared my stories with anyone who will listen because if I don't share what I've experienced, those I love won't realize what's available for them. They will have their own experiences with God, and I believe my sharing gives them the courage and faith to believe God for big things, and I want big things for them!

I want my family and friends to receive the life changing power God gives. I want them to encounter Him in His love, mercy, grace and forgiveness. Why? Because when we experience the power of God, we are never the same; we are being changed into His image, becoming more like Him.

Isn't that the goal of being a Jesus follower? To be like Him?

Today, if you have not experienced His power, just ask. He will hear and answer because He desires to impact your life as the two of you experience relationship. May you be blessed with a God-encounter today!

Day 90

The Great Exchange

Deuteronomy 16-17 / Luke 9:7-27 / Psalm 72 / Proverbs 12:8-9

There was so much I could have written about today! I had many thoughts and questions as I read through the verses. Should I talk about the fact that each king was to hand-copy God's instructions and read it daily? Should I talk about Jesus's model of leadership in that He blessed the five loaves and two fish, then gave the food to his trusted disciples to distribute to the people? Should I talk about the value of losing my life for the sake of Christ?

So, you can see my dilemma with such richness in front of me! That said, I'm going to process the fact that the king was to write his own copy of God's law and read it daily as long as he lived. This was to be done so he would learn to fear the Lord and obey all the instructions and decrees. This was to "prevent him from becoming proud and acting as if he is above his fellow citizens."

When I look around at the mess in the world today, it's obvious we've forgotten God's ways. We've forgotten to love the Lord our God with all our hearts and to love our neighbor as ourselves. And these two basic principles, when followed in relationship and love, would solve all the world's problems.

Does that sound too simple? Maybe, but sometimes the simplest truths are the most powerful. There would be less corruption if we loved God and others. Less greed, murder, impurity, but then again, we won't live fully this way until Heaven. We will always have sin to contend with, so what are we to do?

Luke 9:23-25 does come into play after all. "Then he said to the

184

crowd, 'If any of you wants to be my follower, you must give up your own way, take up your cross daily, and follow me. If you try to hang on to your life, you will lose it. But if you give up your life for my sake, you will save it. And what do you benefit if you gain the whole world but are yourself lost or destroyed?'"

Here is a daily task for us in the modern day. The king was to read the words he had written daily, and we are to give up our own way and take up our cross daily. What does it mean to take up your cross?

The words "take up" are defined as "to take upon one's self and carry what has been raised up, to bear. To appropriate what is taken. To take and apply to any use."

"Cross" is defined as "the well-known instrument of most cruel and ignominious punishment" In other words, a place of death.

Do you see in Luke where it says those who try to hang on to their lives will lose them? And that we must give up our lives for His sake. In this way, there is a death of our own way and our own lives, given up for the sake of His way and His life.

My question is, "Have you written down His Words so that you might obey them?" Maybe you haven't written His words, but they must be read and meditated upon daily.

Will you give up what you are doing for the life He planned for you? If it helps, you can think of this process as the adventure of finding His path and plan. I promise it will be filled with the most amazing experiences. We won't have all good things, but His ways will produce His good in us.

185

Day 91

The Earth Belongs to the Lord

Deuteronomy 18-20 / Luke 9:28-50 / Psalm 73 / Proverbs 12:10

There is a thread throughout today's reading that is disturbing, and that is the topic of the wicked, or those who practice evil. I am often reminded that we don't wrestle against flesh and blood (Eph 6:12), and that is true. Our true enemy is but one, the devil.

But we must not forget that just as God has "agents" on earth, which are His people along with the angelic realm, so does satan have agents on earth, which are those who love to do evil. This includes both human and evil angelic forces.

I realize this is a heavy topic, but with all that's happening around us, I believe it's important to be aware and to operate in discernment, so we know how to respond in days such as this. As hard as it is to fathom, there are people around us who love evil, who are tools of the devil.

I still believe most people are good and want to do what's right. Most of us would rather work our jobs, take care of our families, go to church and be left alone. I get that, and I understand not wanting to pick a fight or even to enter a battle, especially if it's not our battle.

But in general, what is the responsibility of the body of Christ when it comes to defending ourselves, our families and our friends against the schemes of the evil one and those he uses to do evil? It's a great question, and one I feel we must explore. I won't be able to fully address this, but I have some thoughts!

Thankfully, we no longer live in Old Testament times when the people of God were instructed to wipe out the nations they

186

were dispossessing from the Promised Land God was giving them. They weren't just being mean in wiping them out. Yes, I'm aware I'm talking about killing and that's not an easy subject. I also would not want to participate in the killing of another.

God told His people to rid the land of those who were practicing evil things. If you want to know what type of evil things, feel free to read Deuteronomy 18:10-14.

In Luke 9:44 it says, "The Son of Man is going to be betrayed into the hands of his enemies."

The word enemies can also be translated as "men". But let's note that the men Jesus was handed over to did not believe He was the Son of God, and they were intent on murdering Him. They were working against Him because they did not understand who He was.

In Psalm 73 we read about the proud, or those who speak only evil and, in their pride, seek to crush others. They are referred to as wicked people.

The word "wicked" is defined as "morally wrong; concretely, an (actively) bad person; condemned, guilty, ungodly, wicked (man), that did wrong."

So, what are we to do? We may or may not encounter truly wicked people personally, but they are certainly affecting our nation and our world. God has a plan for this world, but so does satan. God wants to save His people and satan wants to destroy all he can.

Once we're aware that evil exists and those who are evil are actively fighting against God's plan, how do we respond? Once we are aware of the problem, we must operate in our authority in Christ, the most powerful of which is to use that authority in prayer. Before we pray, we must put on our spiritual armor.

Please read through Ephesians 6:10-18 and put your armor on, preparing yourself for the battle of prayer. Here is some inspiration as you pray.

1 Thessalonians 5:16-18 states, "Always be joyful. Never stop praying. Be thankful in all circumstances, for this is God's will for you who belong to Christ Jesus."

And keep on praying, do not give up, do not allow yourself to be distracted or tired. God's Spirit will sustain you as you ask for your eyes to be opened and that your strength would be renewed.

Isaiah 40:31 states, "But those who trust in the Lord will find new strength. They will soar high on wings like eagles. They will run and not grow weary. They will walk and not faint."

There is no time for fear. There is no time for complaining or excuses, because we have a plan. There is no time for claiming to be unaware because now you know.

A few weeks ago, I ran across a phrase in a Jim Caviezel video that stood out to me. It said, "God woke you up for a reason." And that He has.

I'm standing, I'm praying, I'm not giving up on the plan God has for me and for this world. After all, I am His and the world is His!

"The earth is the Lord's and the fullness thereof."
—Psalm 24:1-3

Biography

Maria Kear began her Jesus journey when she received Christ at the age of five. That dramatic encounter with Him set her up for a life filled with a spiritual hunger that compels her to not only seek after God wholeheartedly, but also to create hunger and thirst in others through her words, experience and life example.

Maria and her husband Jeff have three adult children and as of this writing they have four grandchildren with more promised in the future.

Maria and Jeff launched a house church called Bethesda Springs House of Mercy and Grace in July 2020 when the Lord surprised them with His plans as they fasted and prayed just prior.

Maria has many fond sayings, one of which is, "I want to leave this earth with my hair still on fire!"

May your "hair" catch fire as you read and become hungrier for Him.

189